In Search of
What Lies Beneath

Dr. Sharon Stone

ISOWLB@aol.com

PRESS

THE DEDICATION

This writing is dedicated to my future husband who is not here yet, but coming into view! I am the manifestation of your special made-to-order request and heart's desire. This was written with you in mind because I wanted to be sure I was a good thing before you found me and not because you found me. It is my responsibility to become your kind words long before you speak them. Therefore, I endeavored to search for what lied beneath the superficial thinking of my self, eradicate anything that would hinder our oneness, and to discover the powerful, loving, caring, and giving person whom God first, created for Himself and then secondly, made for you. I am the refined dust of your created bone, made just for you. Conclusively, it is not enough for me to be a woman - I must also be a Lady for I am a whole contribution to your whole life. And until you find me, I'll be ready.

Thank you:

Mayor John Washington
"For the many laughs, your business mind, and that there is only one way to do things."

Howard O. Jameson, Ph.D.
"My spiritual father. You are the reason I study so much! Oh, that I might know Him. Thank you for trusting the gift of teaching in me."

Evangelist Dr. Dorothy McBride
"My spiritual mother. I want to be like the Christ in you when I grow up!"

Pastor Bruce C. Lester, Sr.
"Thank you for constantly reminding me 'The devil is a liar!'"

Pastors Renae McClaine and Timothy Smith
"This is the evidence of your word of knowledge; the revealing secret of my heart."

Linda Stone
"Although God is new to you, you are not new to Him! Be encouraged - He already knows."

Iola Randall
"My 6 a.m. prayer partner. Your love for life and faith in God has left a mark on me."

Kenny Dawson
"Your audacious energy is encouraging and contagious."

Gladys Carden
"You always said 'yes' and 'keep'em coming'."

All JSM students from whom I've learned so much
"Thanks for everything. I pray there's something written on these pages that reminds you that you belong to Him."

To my friends and family far and near (you know who you are), *"Thanks for the push!"*

Dear God

"You are the only one I know that knows all about me and still loves me. For this,

I Love You!
I Honor You!
I Worship You!
I Serve You!
I Thank You!"

WHAT'S IT ALL ABOUT?

If what you see is what you get, then what do you see? Is it possible to see and not know; know yet be misinformed?

When the emphasis is placed on the superficial, the obvious, or what's in front of us, there is a slender yet sometimes strong tendency to allow what we *can* see to carry more weight than what we cannot. We allow what we superficially see, to be the truth. Basically, we allow the cover to dictate the content or the container determines, even predicts, the substance. Yet, most often, we're disappointed with the result because the content didn't meet our expectations. Superficial or surface thinking and seeing gives us expectations of the substance or content and when we realize what we thought or saw superficially misrepresented the substance, we then have disappointment to deal with and trust becomes an issue. It is difficult to trust the substance when we find out we've been misinformed by its cover; when we've found out they were not who they portrayed themselves to be. The portrayal was a betrayal.

Kind words, a tailored suit and tie for him, a clean cut and fancy car should not be the all-inclusive determining factors of who he really is. They are part of his cover but not the conclusion of his substance or content. They are fact but may not be truth. Likewise, a tailored suit or fine dress for her, gorgeous hair, manicured nails, and a beautiful smile don't tell the real story of her. Truth is, we can look the part, get the part and never get to keep the part. The substance of who we really are is the gold of who we are. Because everything that glitters is not gold, it's the gold of ourselves we should seek and discover, not the temporal satisfaction of what glitters. What glitters can sometimes fool us into thinking it is something that it's not. You'll be able to tell however, when what you think is gold is placed in an environment or comes in contact with a substance stronger and contradicting than or to itself. The surface then will change, revealing the content, what it really is; brass! - A substance capable of losing its luster. But solid gold never does.

If little or no energy is given to search for *what lies beneath*, even for ourselves, we can become complacent and comfortable with the cover and what we think (fact) and never tap into the substance of what is (truth). We spend a great deal of time and money maintaining our cover or the container but not enough time getting to know our content, the substance, the truth of who we really are. It's the substance of humanity that makes a difference in life. It is the substance of who we are that has the most effective impact on life.

Contributory tools for successful living of this life come from our substance. A man or woman can be chosen for a job based on how they dress for the interview. However, if the employer later terminates for unethical behavior, insubordination, excessive tardiness, or non-productive performance, then simply put, the cover was a misrepresentation of the substance. When we realize our cover should be indicative and the forerunner of our content - who we really are, the more successful we will be in our family, church, employment, community, society, and nation.

If we don't know who we really are, we cannot live meaningful lives nor be happy with our whole self because something will always be missing and enough will never really be enough. We can be pleased with ourselves externally, but internally, we're hurting. Internally, we've buried issues we would much rather stay buried. Internally, we don't know why we exist. If we accept the challenge of facing what lies beneath head-on, we will no doubt, discover potential we didn't know we had that causes us to know why we exist and gives us a right to live.

If our purpose is unknown to ourselves, how can we know the value of self-worth? If our potential is never discovered, what then is our contribution to that self-worth, our family, church, society and community, employer, or nation? If our integrity and character is never challenged to develop, how can wholeness and balance be obtained? What then, about vision, patience, wisdom, love, and understanding? These great tools of life are what lie beneath the superficial. They seek to materialize themselves in our life, helping to make us into something this world cannot live without – men and women of substance; that is, purpose and potential.

Throughout the remainder of this writing, I've attempted to write about areas in our life we must face head on, deal with, get over, and move away from, literally and emotionally, in order to move forward. God has placed within us the ability to be and do all He has created us to be and do. It lies within us and beneath what we see about ourselves superficially. God wants who He has created us to be, to radiate, affecting everything we do and the lives of each other. The male needs the female, the female needs the male and they both need God, their Creator. Some chapters of this writing combine a short story and complementing poetry while in others the poem alone is free form and tells the story.

When you can *see* what has been said then what has been said has just knocked on the door of your understanding. This, my friend, is the beginning of discovering potential. Potential houses your ability to be changed in your thinking and ultimately your actions, making a difference, positively affecting this life with the essence and substance of who you really are. To know what you house is to know purpose. The ability to produce what you house is potential. To actually produce what you house is to be fruitful. To increase what you produce is to multiply. Be fruitful and multiply!

It is my sincere desire and prayer for you that somewhere within the content of this writing, you will find hope, encouragement, motivation, and inspiration for change. Then, you are positioned to help someone else.

THE FOREWORD

D r. Sharon Stone has written a masterpiece of literary prose and poetry in "In Search of What Lies Beneath".

Her incisive and perspicuous view of the hidden and unknown doubtless is the product of the leading of the Holy Spirit.

As a godly woman of letters and deep spiritual insight, Dr. Stone here has enunciated and elucidated precious biblical truths, and has artfully and skillfully applied them to the vicissitudes of every day life.

May you be enriched, enhanced, embellished and edified as you peruse the profound verities and sublime beauty of this work of literary art.

Howard O. Jameson, Ph.D.
Jameson Schools of Ministry and Theology, and
International Evangelism Association

THE PROLOGUE

Where is the Love?

How do I love thee? Let me count the ways![1] No other word is more widely used or said yet so little understood and misrepresented, than love. Were did it come from and what does it mean? How do I love in times like these and considering all that has happened to me, how *can* I love? One must make an effort to understand the truth about love before one can know how to love and more importantly why one should love.

Although there are many definitions, expressions, and acts of love, its foundational truth can only be made clear from knowledge of the Creator of love. Further, this knowledge broadens our horizons and enables us to see the bigger picture. Knowledge of the Creator of love gives us an awareness of purpose. That is, who am I and why on earth am I here, in this place, in this relationship, in this neighborhood, in this church, at this particular place of employment, at this school or college, in this country?

Every individual's purpose for life is an expression and gift of the love of God to life itself. Every individual who fulfills God's purpose for their life is literally saying and doing what God would say and do in that place, that home, that family, that church, that community, that place of employment, school or college, that nation. Humanity is to be the ambassador for God. We represent Him in every area of our life, each, contributing to the wholeness of life itself.

Everyone is important to God for we were created by Him *for* Him and He has therefore, given us the potential and ability to be exactly what He has created us to be; nothing more and certainly, nothing less. You are not a replica of any other human! Even identical twins have individual purpose with God.

Each chapter of this writing with the use of poetry and in some areas, Bible reference, will discuss some aspect of the foundational love of God and how we can build on that love and why we should reciprocate the love first shown to us. If you find yourself having experienced anything this writing speaks of, you have experienced the love of God for you, because you are still living. He didn't allow what happened to you to totally destroy you. You are therefore, still alive to tell it. You must now reciprocate His love to you by loving Him with your life that He spared. It is the love first shown to us that empowers us to in-turn love ourselves, God, and others. Each chapter of this collection of thoughts is an eye exercise, written to provoke thoughts of the mind's eye.

I once learned natural vision doesn't just include the eyes but the brain, mind, and body also. In using the concept of 3D vision (three dimensions), magnificently, the brain and the mind have the capability of allowing you to see embedded images beyond the surface image as well as giving flat images depth. Each eye sees the same image but from different angles and capturing additional slightly different information. When these two images arrive at the back of the brain simultaneously, the mind, processing and interpreting, combines all the similar information and then adds the differences to form one picture.

Amazingly, those small differences create a bigger final picture of synergy, where the result is greater than the sum of its parts. This final picture is 3D having depth, height, and width. It seems to leap off the surface and suspend itself in mid-air. If the image is hidden, what you were able to see superficially now becomes the wallpaper for the suspended image that comes to the forefront. Likewise, if the image is not hidden but visible with surface or superficial viewing, using the same 3D concept, the image still comes to the forefront while everything else is like a backdrop, putting a noticeable space between the image and its background; the image floats. In either case, 3D vision allows you to see what you will never be able to see just looking at the surface. It adds another dimension. However, in order to see 3D images, you must train the eye to look beyond what it sees superficially. It requires constant and consistent focus. It's as if you say to your brain "take me beyond what I can see and show me what I cannot see." So it is with life. It is not about what we can see on the surface but what your brain and mind have the ability to see beneath that surface. This is potential. God has already provided vision for your life but it has no depth, width, or height (no substance or synergy) to you without first discovering your potential or ability to see beyond what you can see, in order to materialize what you cannot see.

In the search of what lies beneath what we see of our self, we will find the footings upon which our life is built, made of the love of God, in 3D. It has depth, it has height, and it has width. It seeks to leap off the pages of life and suspends itself in mid air and become obvious. God's love is a synergetic picture – a picture just as great as the sum of its parts. We know this because we've seen the power of love create and strengthen families, heal hearts, bring hope, build communities, change minds, decisions and nations.

As the footings of a house support the entire structure of the house, so it is with love in our life. Love was initiated and introduced by God to support the entire life structure of mankind. We in turn, must be careful how and what we attempt to build upon those footings of love. There is therefore, a blueprint for building the house or the life of mankind.

As the stability of a house is determined by the strength of its footings, the stability of our life is determined by the strength of its footings. Every area of the house expresses the strength of the entire house. Every area of our life should express the overall strength of our life, all based on the foundational footings of love. Imagine how strong we, our families, communities, schools and colleges, employers, and nation would be if when building, its foundation was love!

It is my desire that you find some aspect of your life depicted somewhere throughout the pages of this reading and conclude that even though peculiar and negative things have happened, trouble seemed to have always been at your door, and the windows of your life are more dirty on the inside than on the outside, God still loves you and it was not His love that caused these things but rather humanity's ignorance to His love. And because of His love, purpose and potential for our life, we're still here. The love of God can give us the power to see in 3D, who we really are, by enabling us to look beyond the surface and even beyond those things we keep suppressed, eradicating what has been suppressed, and then coming forth as gold in its purist state.

Ignorance is a state or condition of being uneducated, unaware, or uniformed about any subject matter. Freedom from the past is to understand why it happened in the first place. Once educated or informed about its root cause, that knowledge can empower us to be free from that history repeating itself in our life. The fact is the knowledge but we must do something with that knowledge. Go beyond the fact and get to the truth because knowledge of the truth makes us free. We can then utilize the story of our past to help others who may find themselves in the same negative and some-times devastating and life-changing situations.

Realize your life was built on the foundational Spirit-lead purpose of God and its footings that support it are made of the love of God; A sure foundation. Follow the obvious winding path to journey phases of life beginning with God's amazing grace gone unrecognized and ending with freedom so free, it doesn't discriminate and therefore, comes in any color; colors that together are the rainbow of promise.

I peeped in the cave of life
And as far as I could see
Was all this love
Waiting for me

It'll never run out
No one can have too much
When you live by love
All life is touched.

Enjoy!

THE CONTENT

CHAPTER 1
AMAZING GRACE 25

Progress is Good…in the Right Direction! 27
When Things Look Bad, Look Again! 32
You Make Me Smile 34
God Is 37
We Hold These Truths 40
Amazing Grace 41

CHAPTER 2
IN THE NAME OF LOVE, BE HEALED! 43

The Power of Touch 45
He Touched Me 48
Steele Magnolias in a Black Vase 50
The Skin I'm In Has Sinned 51
My Suitcase Has Wheels 53
B.A.D. 54
God is Greater than My Pain 57
God is Greater 60
The Rain Made Everything Grow But Me 63
Singing in the Rain 68
It Ain't Gonna Reign No More 71

CHAPTER 3
A CONTRIBUTION TO THE WHOLE 73

I Am What He's Missing *75*
That's My Momma *81*
I Am My Mother's Daughter *83*
Hello, My Name is Unknown *83*
More than a Woman (The Challenge) *89*
More than a Woman (Poem - part I) *92*
More than a Woman (Poem - part II) *94*
More than a Woman (Poem - part III) *96*
Set the Table *101*
Cryin' in the Dark *103*
What If *105*

CHAPTER 4
COLOR ME FREE! 109

You Made Me Smile...Again! *110*
My Eyes Said "No!" *114*
Got No Time *116*
Running for Nothing *117*
A Wealthy Place *120*
I'm Already Dead! *121*
Finally...I Asked *123*
Queen of Sheba *125*

CHAPTER 5
BECAUSE I LOVE HIM 127

In Thee Oh Lord *128*
These Bones Shall Live *130*
Kissing God with My Life *132*
Remember to Forget *134*

CHAPTER 6
WELL DONE! 137

My Light *138*
Wine from a Seedless Grape *139*
I Had a Baby Last Night! *142*
Where Is The Church? *145*
Some Glad Mornin'! *148*
Until *151*
Grandmom Said *153*

CHAPTER 7
ADAM, WHERE ART THOU? 155

A Special Order...Worth the Weight *157*
Lord, I'm Ready to Order *158*
For Me? *163*
The Man I See *165*
I Met A Man *168*
There's a Man in the Kingdom *172*

CONCLUSION 175

CHAPTER 1

Amazing Grace

"The use of the word amazing denotes humanity's promulgated attempt to label something far beyond its natural ability to comprehend."

PROGRESS IS GOOD...IN THE RIGHT DIRECTION!

IT WAS A WET, dreary, and gray day as I sat in the airport, waiting to board a plane for a business trip. I watched through the over sized window and stared at the occasional thunder and lightening and concluded the weather was too bad to fly. Surely this flight would be cancelled.

My anticipation of a cancellation caused me to strategize and prepare my next steps. I was an analyst. What would I need to do should this flight be cancelled? There were many intercom announcements of many delays; however, none gave heed to my expected cancellation. Would the flight's delay graduate to a denial? While I continued to think on my plan of action – just in case – the announcement was made to begin boarding my flight.

Isn't it funny, the quick choices and decisions we make when the thought of alternative choices inconvenience us? It was easier for me to board the plane then to carry out my alternative that took a heaping 20 minutes to plan! It involved re-routing and taking a connection flight to my ultimate desti-nation costing more time, money, and inconvenience. But, in spite of my alternative plan orchestrated because of what I thought was to be a cancelled trip, somehow, getting on the plane felt like progress. It was easier to do that then to deal with the inconvenience associated with my alternative plan.

Even if take-off is delayed, at least I'm on board. Progress - right? Isn't that what life's all about?

Sometimes in our life, what we think should be cancelled, removed, done away with, or denied, is not the plan. As is my trip, there's a plane you may need to board in spite of what's going on around and in your life. Get on board; in spite of what you see, you're making progress. Stay the course, stay focused. In spite of how you feel, you're making progress. The plane and the plan are controlled by God, the ultimate Source and Resource who will ensure a safe arrival. Sometimes God will not change *what* you can see and feel but He'll change *how* what you see and feel affects you. Progress is good but only in the right direction!

I boarded the plane. I was comfortable and the plane began to taxi the runway – just a little behind schedule. But I didn't concern myself with that because in relation to my expected cancellation and alternative plan, I was making progress. It's thundering and lightening, raining, and grey skies were getting darker seemingly by the second. It no longer mattered to me. I was on board, we are moving, and I was making progress.

Progression in the right direction is evidence of realized purpose. Whatever your purpose in life, there must be focus and progression to that end. There is no good success or fulfillment of life without the fulfillment of the purpose for life. Once we realize what God's divine purpose is for our life, we should have testimonies about the progression and the necessary actions we took, in order to encourage and help someone else progress in the right direction.

With a deep sigh of relief, I closed my eyes to enjoy the comfort of that relief. I comforted myself with my own thoughts: I'm making progress. I may get their late, but I'll get there. And when I do, I don't believe I'll miss out on anything because I didn't cause this storm. I didn't cause the delay. If I didn't cause it, then God allowed it and whatever

He allows, is alright with me. As part of my self-comfort, I reminded myself, God is too wise to make a mistake and even if that were possible, and He did, who could know it? Who could help God recover from His own mistake? Who could tell Him He made a mistake? If He could make a mistake, He's not God. I comforted myself with these thoughts as the plane began to take off. I smiled with the thought - I'm making progress!

Now in the air, we're experiencing terrible turbulence. The plane, as large as it is, feels like a toy against the storm. But making progress in the right direction is a comforting thought. I'm comforted that the storm did not stop the flight; however, I find something else I think I should now be concerned about. I couldn't help but start to think if the entire trip would be like this. I had no alternative plan for this! I'm in the air and I had no choice but to endure.

> How long do I have to go through this?
> It's not pleasant in this place.
> It's uncomfortable in this place.
> It's disturbing in this place.
> I can't see in this place.
> How long?

Nonetheless, I'm making progress and in the right direction! Just when I thought about voicing my irrelevant opinion, the pilot begins to give information but for me, it was a message from God.

"Good evening Ladies and Gentlemen. This is your pilot speaking. We are experiencing some turbulence at this altitude and are unable to turn off the 'fasten your seatbelt' sign. Please keep your seatbelts on for a few more moments. We are obtaining clearance to increase our altitude where we can then fly above the storm. Please, remain seated until such time at which we will inform you by turning off the 'fasten your seatbelt' sign and you will be free to move about. Thank you for your patience."

The words from the pilot came with its' own comfort. We heard what he said and took refuge in his words. Not long afterward, I could feel the elevation of the plane and watched through the window during the elevation process. Someone had given the requested clearance. I could make sense of nothing I saw. It was like flying through massive gray smoke. The pilot could not see anything either but was totally reliant on radar and any instructions from nearby towers. The plane was in fact, being directed and guided from sources out of his control which obligated his obedience.

We continued to soar on a slight angle upward experiencing what felt a lot like an automobile hitting pot holes, but in the air.

> How long will this thing last?
> When am I coming out?
> When is it going to be over?
> What does it come to talk about?

I closed my eyes and before I knew it, I felt warmth over my eyelids and brightness beneath them. I opened my eyes. It was sunny and bright and the clouds looked like huge soft cotton pillows. It was peaceful. It was beautiful. It was bright. It was calm. I smiled with relief. The storm was not behind us, it in fact was beneath us!

When I personalized the experience, I concluded, what was before me that tried to hinder me is now beneath me. It made me smile again. I'm making progress, I thought - in my natural and spiritual life. But what did it come to talk to me about? Why was the experience necessary? God through that experience taught me how to live above people, things, and situations in my life. Not in arrogance but rather deliverance. He had already provided the clearance for this to be possible. God is the Director of our life and His instructions obligates our obedience. No matter how difficult the path may be sometimes, we can take refuge in His words and find comfort and peace.

Everything we're delivered from is not only behind us, labeled as part of our past, but they should also be beneath us. It's no longer a desire to do those things because it's beneath our character to do them. It's not conducive to who we really are. When you give your life to God, He will deliver you from the hurts and pain of people and situations, grant a clearance that elevates you above what you're going through, and cause you to experience a peace you cannot explain. You will not feel like you deserve it. But He'll give it to you anyway because He loves you.

What do you feel God has placed within you to do but you're denying? Why do you have an alternative plan? Our denial of Him causes delays of a progressive life. How will you handle the delay? What about the intermediate choices you now have to make because of the delay you've brought on yourself? Progress is good but only in the right direction.

WHEN THINGS LOOK BAD, LOOK AGAIN!

What it looks like ain't necessarily what it is
Sometimes you have to look again
And when you do, take a closer look
To what lies beneath and within

What you don't see the first time
May require a second look
Don't go by the superficial
It most often is a crook

Who wants to divert your attention
To the thing that hurts the most
Neglecting the *source* of the pain
That lies within you to boast

What it looks like ain't necessarily what it is
It may be hard to believe
Unsure about what you're looking at?
Don't be deceived

Try the spirit by the Spirit
The strongest one will stand
The other will utterly have to fall
By the Stronger One's right hand

Whenever things look bad
Simply look again
What lies beneath what you see
Is the Source of the win

God has a better perspective
Looking at it from His view
Talk to Him about what you see
He'll share his view with you

When you can't see with your own eyes
Look through the eyes of God
He'll light your path and guide your feet
With a simple nod

He'll show you where the problem lies
And what it comes to do
When you see it with the eyes of God
You'll know just what to do

Sometimes the road really is rough
And you'll feel like you can't win
But whenever times do look that bad?
Close your eyes, smile, and look again!

YOU MAKE ME SMILE

I smell your sweet aroma
that blesses my air
when the wind blows
through my hair.
Jasmine,
you
make me smile.

Skies are grey
throughout the day
but not disturbed
you
blossom anyway.
Jasmine,
You make me smile.

Your scent is attracting
drawing attention
to evening guests
who've come to mention,
Jasmine,
makes me smile.

Your leaves
ever green
rich and full of color
shine in the light
of day and night.
Jasmine,
you make me smile.

I watch you grow
fast
the white of your garment
lasts
you climb to higher heights
headed for light.
Jasmine,
you make me smile.

You have a counterfeit:
poisonous
deceiving many
a sedative
cunning and canning;
but Jasmine,
only you,
make me smile.

Your oil
touches and perfumes my skin
blends
and cleanses my hair
making me aware
that Jasmine
makes me smile.

My God is like
my Jasmine
to me
He loves
unconditionally
He's my sweet
aromatic wind
that blows
whatever the day holds

continued

He
already knows.
Rich and full of life
Eternal and right
undisturbed
by the light of night.
Helps me grow
removing deterrence
as I head for the Light
of His countenance.
God!
You make me smile.

You too have a counterfeit:
poisonous
deceiving many
a sedative
cunning and canning
destroyed, angry, competitive;
but God!
only You make me smile.

Your oil
touches and perfumes
the skin of my life
Blends
and cleanses my heart
of strife
reminding me
You make me smile.
God! You! Make! Me! Smile!

GOD IS

As big as you allow Him to be
As strong as you reflect Him to be

As bright as you show Him to be
As close as you need Him to be

As powerful as you believe Him to be
As saving as you know Him to be
And more

God Is
Not restricted by many or few
Who He can be…is up to you.

Who He will be is who He is,
Lord of Lords, King of Kings,
Long before the crib.

What you've done and where you've been
Makes no difference to Him.
He'll take it all, have a ball
In showing Satan, he can't win!

In spite of you and me, God is.
Because of you and me,
God will always be,

Who and what we need
Whenever we most need it
Through the self-authenticated Witness,
The Holy Spirit.

continued

To conceive *from* Him
Is an honor of high degree
To bring forth *for* Him
Is like that of the olive tree

Who's roots grow long and strong
And cannot be destroyed.
Bringing forth continual olives for oil
Healing and cleansing what has been soiled.

God is who He says He is
Whether believed or not
Again, He's not restricted
And His plan cannot be stopped.

Faith is the certainty of the essence
of Who God is *now*.
When it's all over and nothing else is said
God will still be around!

He'll never cease to exist
He set that limit on Himself.
So whenever we would need Him
He would be our present help.

God is all you know about Him
And…more.
And living for Him,
Brings great reward.

God is the gold thread that gives
The fabric of our being value.
Since *He* is who He says *He* is,
To thine own self, be true.

What will be will be
What will come, will go
But like the olive tree that brings the oil
Be fruitful and grow!

WE HOLD THESE TRUTHS

A Way Out
A Path of Hope
A Signal Light
A Rope

A Word that Helps
A Song that's sung
A Prayer that's prayed
A new Life begun

We hold these truths
Within our self
To be self-evident
Of internal wealth

Public enemy #1
Me, myself, and I
The Way, the Hope, the Light, the Rope
We need to survive

The Word, the Help, the Song, the Prayer
Commit to keep us strong
We hold these truths, as the proof
We all can get along.

AMAZING GRACE

When He took my hand
And walked me through
I said.... "Amazing!"

When I couldn't choose Him
He said "I've chosen you"
And I said.... "Amazing!"

When I remembered
That He forgot
I said.... "Amazing!"

When I didn't deserve
His unmerited favor
I understood His grace
And changed my behavior
And I said.... "Amazing!"

So unworthy is how I feel
About our relationship
He spends time with me and helps me to see
His grace won't let me quit.
And I say.... "Amazing!"

Amazing Grace shall always be
My sweet song of praise
I say "a-m-a-z-i-n-g!"
When I think of those days.

CHAPTER 2

In the Name of Love,

Be Healed!

"More effort is directed toward suppressing the truth than healing by the truth because inner healing begins with something we're not so ready to do - confess."

THE POWER OF TOUCH

THE SENSE OF TOUCH is one of the five complementing senses used to express and transfer thoughts, feelings, emotions, love, and affection. The sense of touch helps us to realize and understand texture, shapes, sizes, climates or seasons, and feelings.

We begin understanding life in an elementary form, when we're taught shapes, sizes, and texture in pre-school. It helps to develop the creativity and awareness portion of the brain enabling us to find, name, and connect similarities of things. Touch also helps us learn and name the associated feelings that come as a result of what we've touched or what or who has touched us. Without the ability to touch, knowing what it is to *feel* is hardly experienced and makes that person untouchable.

What we want others to know can be expressed by touching. We can get a person's attention by tapping them on the shoulder. Desires are expressed by touch. We can let someone know we love them by hugging them. Adversely, we can let a person know we're angry by hitting them. So, touch is very important in the life of any human being because it's directly attached to the emotional side of all humans and enables us to express what we sometimes find difficult to verbally say. We simply can express many things by touch.

As children, the brains develop through touch, strengthening its memory. The brain remembers what the object felt like when touched by the hands. Likewise, the brain itself, remembers what it felt like to be touched. This memorization is designed to last an eternity. It is the power of touch.

The created man expressed by God, housed feelings for God and the need to be touched by God whether with words or with His physical presence. The woman who was created in the man housed the same needs. However, because she was made from the man – a further process, all the feelings and expressions of the man by God were refined in the woman. So, her feelings are more refined, her need to be touched whether with words or with His presence are refined. The female requires more emotional stability than the man and sensitivity is a natural female trait.

Because the female is more emotional than a male, she remembers and expresses the essence of feelings of touch more than the male. The female has a greater dependency for loving thoughts expressed by touch. It is built into the fiber of her being and evidenced in her making. She was housed by the body of the man before she was made from him. She is used to being encompassed and protected.

When the man was created, he was created with the touch of God and God expressed Himself to the man through that touch. God touched his heart with His, touched his mind with His, and touched his spirit with His. In expressing Himself to the man, God used the sense of touch. His complete purpose for mankind was expressed with His touch. The resulted man was an expression of God's *imagination* with attributes that made him *like* God but not God. Mankind then, was and is an 'expressed' image bearer of God.

The things females need to maintain emotional stability carry more weight than how big the man's house is or what kind of car he drives. She needs to be touched with words and physical presence. Her emotions need attention to detail.

After all, she was touched by God a second time - first, in the *creation* of the male and second, in the *making* of the female. Touch is extremely important to the female. She requires touch and the time it takes to do so because it contributes to the making of who she is. All humanity requires the touch of the one who brought them into this world.

The sense of touch is a powerful tool utilized to express and transfer feelings but when the touch is inappropriate, the feelings are also inappropriate and the spirit behind the inappropriate feelings is inappropriate. The victim of inappropriate touch has to somehow deal with something they may not have lived longed enough to try to comprehend, diagnose, or even speak about. An inappropriate touch to a child affects the life of a child until they are old enough to confront what was inappropriate, demoralize and kill its root. The strength of an inappropriate touch is so powerful that the touch follows the child throughout his/her life and futuristically, makes it difficult to deal with something designed to be as innocent and powerful as the sense of touch.

Inappropriate touch was not part of the creation of man or in the making of the female. It negatively affects the emotions of a child and in particular, the female. Her *refined* feelings are far more fragile than that of the male. I believe an inappropriate touch by one must be counteracted with an appropriate touch by a stronger one in order to regain one's trust with touch.

Knowledge of one's purpose and potential eradicates abuse in any form. The benefit of anything or anyone is realized and experienced only with knowledge of its purpose and potential.

HE TOUCHED ME

Although it's a spiritual song about God
Of great victory and wonderful change
It never at all meant God to me
For God was not his name.

A little child with much knowledge
Beyond the years of my age
My intelligence still couldn't comprehend
Why someone would put me in this cage.

Who do I tell and how?
What will I say if I do?
Certainly someone would understand
Wipe the tears and help me through.

What is this thing called?
Is this how it's supposed to be?
Will somebody ever let me know
They were not supposed to touch me?

A child has a natural ability
To trust and reverence adults
But when that trust is violated
Confusion and hatred result.

I grew up anyway and somehow learned
How *not* to hate
It had to be the love of God
That kept my heart at a steady pace.

When I had a right to be angry
And hate for the rest of my life
It was the love of God that kept me
With assurance He'd make it all right.

I had suppressed the truth about the reality of the song
For it meant something different to me
When they died or moved on, I lived with the memory
Wondering if I'll ever be free.

My smile suppressed the truth every day
From a cage no one but God could see
The little girl's body grew up as it naturally should
But her heart was still wounded with debris.

One day God touched the little girl
Buried inside the woman so deep
Giving her a reason to keep on living
Her soul He promised to keep.

The little girl is all grown up
Transformed from woman to Lady
The cage was unlocked then thrown away
For God touched and set her free.

STEELE MAGNOLIAS IN A BLACK VASE

Beauty, color, shapely, fragrant
Magnolia's ways
Hurt, pain, emotional gain
Steele magnolias
in a black vase

Strong, ever green, shade
Magnolia's gaze
Strong but wrong yet full of life
Steele magnolias
in a black vase

Stately, upright, durable, elegant
Magnolias…winter's crave
Weak, fragile, winter's foe
Steele magnolias
in a black vase

Smooth, soft, complementing cream
Magnolia's days
Tough, powerful, liquid vanilla
Steele magnolias
in a black vase
yet still.

THE SKIN I'M IN HAS SINNED

The skin I'm in has sinned
Left me ashamed and condemned
No knowledge of restoration
No reason for celebration
of the salvation of my soul
I am lost.

Where can I go?
Who do I talk to
About me
About you
And what we should do?
Because the skin I'm in
has sinned
and has
no clue.

Forgive me Lord,
for I have sinned
and hid myself
from the shame within.
Cleanse me
Cover me
Set me free
from the nerve of myself
to wanna be
free to be
who I think I am
versus the woman you
know
see
and purposed to be.

continued

The skin I'm in
has sinned
But God
has made it possible
for me
to begin
again.
And I thank Him.

My Suitcase Has Wheels

Let it go
Too heavy to carry
Too easy to drag
Let it go

So many pieces, so easy to drag
Are the cares of life sometime
What should be an enjoyable trip
Too many times has me crying

Trying not to take so much baggage
As I travel on my life's journey
Let it go, turn it loose, let God be
My defense Attorney

I have a right to remain silent - a right to an attorney
He has been appointed to me
Whatever the charges against my life
My Attorney for me, will plead

Watch what you carry in your suitcase on wheels
Carry nothing you know you won't need
Should a search be required and your suitcase is opened
What would they see, how would you plead?

Let it go
Too heavy to carry
Too easy to drag
Let it go

B.A.D.

A reflection of a maternity ward visit
Where all the newborns were placed
I couldn't help but wonder
What in life they would face.

This one was born with a thick black crown
And eyes wide shut to life
He grew up to be a brilliant physician
And took an attorney to be his wife.

She was born with golden blonde hair
Each smooth wavy lock marked her potential
She never married but still in life,
She was extremely influential.

Taking care of business in a big city
This one sits in a government position
Seeds of God were implanted in her
And had come into fruition.

And this one when born,
Cried continuously days after
Could it be a sign he knew
This world had lost its laughter?

This woman had yellow juntas
When she was born
But today she's a gorgeous model
With skin like Lena Horne.

This young man was premature
Not expected to live
Look at him now, a billionaire
With plenty of surplus to give!

The Doctor said, this one would live
But never be able to walk
She proved him wrong when she walked the stage
Prepared to give her talk.

This one born with thumb in mouth
A sign of self sufficiency
Today he received the humanitarian award
Spent millions just meeting needs.

And this one here, they said was so early
Would die with the brain underdeveloped
But the parents said "Not so, my child
Will not only live, but tell it."

It's a shame these contributions to life
Are locked up in my head
'Cause looking around, I can't help but see
Why the cribs are empty…
these **Babies Are Dead**!

GOD IS GREATER THAN MY PAIN

IN THESE TROUBLED TIMES of much uncertainty, pain, and disappointment, it can sometimes be difficult, for some, to believe or even feel that there is a loving and caring God concerned about us and what happens in our life. Sometimes, the pain is simply too great and the burden far too heavy that it cripples our ability to see or feel anything beyond the current pain or heaviness.

The conceptual idea of an all-mighty, all-knowing, all-powerful God being concerned and caring about a mere human having faults, weaknesses, and mistakes, can at times, seem out-of-reach and even unobtainable. However, the Bible teaches that God is very much concerned about the life of mankind simply because we were created *by* Him, *for* Him. "For I know the thoughts I think toward you, saith the Lord, thoughts of peace, and not evil, to give you an expected end." (Jeremiah 29:11). No matter what mistakes we've made or what wrong we've done in the past, He is willing to forgive, heal, prosper, and grant us peace with a certainty and an assurance of His love for us.

In order to be free and relieved from pain that affects the natural body, a physician must prescribe something greater than the actual pain. This same principle applies with God.

Healing, restoration and relief from our pain and hurts lie in the acknowledgement and acceptance of a God who is **greater** than the actual pain and able to heal, restore and relieve us from it. "...cannot I do with you as the potter? saith the Lord. Behold, as the clay is in the potter's hand, so are ye in my hand..." (Jeremiah 18:6)

We may be broken, torn, weak, no knowledge of purpose, no sense of direction, feeling unloved and unable to love others. But God, like the skilled potter with a ball of clay, it too having the same types of characteristics and needs, will take us in His hands and carefully and uniquely mold and make us. He will restore our life, make us strong, give us shape, direction, and make known to us purpose, love and the ability to love others. He will do all according to His perfect plan for our life. There is absolutely nothing too hard for God. "Behold, I am the Lord, the God of all flesh: is there any thing too hard for me? (Jeremiah 32:27)

Acknowledgement and acceptance of the only true and living God and His Son makes us one of His children. Therefore, no matter what we go through, when we call on Him, He delights *and* finds pleasure in answering our call. When we seek Him, He will let us find Him. When we knock, He will open the door. "Then shall ye call upon me, and ye shall go and pray unto me, and I will hearken unto you. And ye shall seek me, and find me, when ye shall search for me with all your heart. And I will be found of you, saith the Lord..." (Jeremiah 29:12-14).

There is nothing that has or can ever happen to us that God cannot love us through. There is nothing His love cannot cleanse us from. He unequivocally and unconditionally loves us. There is no place so low or high His love cannot reach. He is greater than your hurts and pain and even your needs, wants, and desires. He is magnificent in all His ways and His love for us is the antidote for the cares and pain of this life.

God has the ability to see beyond what He hears me say. My pain sometimes won't allow me to express what I'm really feeling because my mind can't seem to interpret the pain in my heart. As it tries, I speak but sometimes even the words I say don't justify the degree of hurt. So God looks directly at my heart, interprets my tears and tells me it's alright that I don't know what to say, He understands.

GOD IS GREATER

He's greater than the pain I felt
When I lost my job
He's greater than the anger I felt
When on the way home I was robbed.

He's greater than the darkness
Experienced whenever I lost sight
He's greater than the hunger I felt
When the money was tight.

He's greater than the hatred I felt
When touched inappropriately
He's greater than the evil that followed
To bring confusion sexually.

He's greater than the piercing words
That came from family members
He's greater than the jealous bones
Sought to put me asunder.

He's greater than the boss
Who hated the color of my skin
He's greater than the distance felt
Without and within.

He's greater than the mistakes I've made
That made him hang his head
And even on the day he did,
He opened His heart and said,

"I'm greater than your midnight hour -
Darkest hour of the day
I'm greater than your not knowing
What to do or what to say.

I'm greater than anything
You'll ever need to face
I'm greater because I'm Self Existing-
Creator of human race.

There's nothing you'll ever go through
I don't already know about
Hold my hand and trust what I say
I will bring you out.

Sometimes I'll take your hand snatching
you out of things
Other times I'll take you through the pain
One thing for sure I'll never let go
Be sure and do the same.

I'm greater than your biggest problem
Greater than your biggest need
I'm greater than any thing or book
You'll ever know or get to read.

I'm greater than your tithe
Greater than your gift
I'm greater than My call on your life
The enemy wants to sift.

I'm greater than the doctor's report
Greater than any medicine
I'll repeat what I said in My love letter to the world
"Now, let's begin"

continued

I'm Alpha and Omega
The beginning and the end
I never start until I'm finished
It's the proof that you win!

Whatever I've started in your life
I'm big enough to complete
I'm not in your life to lose you
I'm in it to make it sweet.

In spite of what you go through here
I'm greater than any of it
Remember I am Self-Existing
Father, Son, and the Holy Spirit.

THE RAIN MADE EVERYTHING GROW BUT ME

IT WAS A BEAUTIFUL MORNING and the sun seemed to promise me it would provide light and comfortable warmth all day. I knew today would be a day I could work in my flower garden. It had been a hot and dry season in early summer and the fruits of my labor had been threatened by no promise of rain. But recently, there was a heavy rain storm, lasting several days. It seemed as though the rain came to make up for lost time or perhaps to apologize for not being there when it was needed the most.

Three days of consistent drenching rain had left behind weeds I never planted, creating more than usual work to do. The beauty of my garden although with obvious growth, was tainted with something I didn't cause but was forced to deal with - weeds. I spent the morning hours removing weeds that had found residence in my flower garden around the trees and shrubs, distorting all its beauty. It made me think, such is life.

I started thinking about my own life and the many things I've had to deal with that were not my fault. You could never tell by looking at me; I made sure of that. My surface or superficial look was designed to keep you from looking beneath it. I thought about the many babies, children, teenagers, and young men and women who are victims of an environment or circumstance they didn't choose. Somewhere, someone was born with a cocaine addiction. This is obviously not there fault yet it has left them to deal with the result of someone else's actions and choices. That same child now has a learning deficiency because the brain was damaged or under-developed. The fathers that never claimed to be fathers have left their sons and daughters with feelings of neglect and rejection. The mother of those same children, are left with trying to figure out how to live with those feelings of neglect and rejection not to mention physical and mental abuse. Some children grew up among the less fortunate and were popular in school for all the wrong reasons leaving somebody's son or daughter with low self-esteem, a power that seeks to destroy knowledge of one's purpose.

I took special note that although there were various kinds of weeds, all were troublesome and absolutely demanded my attention, time, and different ways of removal. Some were superficial and although could be removed with one simple plucking up with the hand, were plentiful and tedious. Other types required tools especially made for the removal of stubborn and deep rooted debris. No matter what the method, all required a degree of my strength, self-will and determination. My flowers need restoration. My life needs restoration.

My attempts to clean this garden generated a chain of thoughts and my mind grew wings that took me on a journey to the past. A past over which I thought I had grown up and away from. A past housing negative attributes I didn't know still existed within me.

For many, life even before birth came with bags full of things they never shopped or asked for. Yet, they feel stuck with having to deal with them and their effects on their life. The flash cards of our life are not always pleasant to visit but our ability to over come is.

I toiled in this garden with undying effort to restore its hidden beauty. There was absolutely no way I would allow what I didn't cause, to overtake the fruits of my labor. The fruit of my labor brings smiles and waves from passer-byes and motivates others to labor for their own beauty. The fruit of my labor encourages others. The fruit of my labor silently tells others they can make it. The beauty of my garden was hidden by what rain caused to grow. I refused to allow the fruit of my labor to be overtaken by weeds and grass I didn't plant. Things I wasn't responsible for. They were intruders.

There has been much rain in my life and I've grown but why haven't I grown up? How can rain touch the outside, nourish and cleanse the inside and cause everything to grow up, blossom, and stand erect but me? The beauty of who I am should be seen as an encouragement for someone else. Why am I wasting time camouflaging debris from the past that has fortified itself so deep, I've learned to live with it? Why have I learned to live with it? What beauty of me cannot be seen because of it? What tools am I going to need to remove it? Am I strong enough to do it? What will I look like when I'm done?

My mind's eye paused at mental flash cards of my life and no doubt the life of others. Each card came from a street called Deep and with its own residential headline address. They spoke to my memory and were resuscitated. They read:

1. 'He Touched Me'. The words that never meant Jesus. No one lives here but *abuse* – a weed.
2. 'Who Am I?' The question no one had ever been able to answer. No one lives here but *uncertainty* – a weed.
3. 'Why Me?' The question that should be answered with 'Why Not Me?' No one lives here but *self-pity* – a weed.
4. 'What is status quo anyway?' Something you've never been. No one lives here but *difference* –a weed.

5. 'She touched Me' The confessed and exposed words for which excuses were made. No one lives here but *hatred* – a weed.
6. 'Failures'. The word that taught the meaning of alone. No one lives here but *fear and doubt* – weeds.
7. 'Jealousy'. The word that taught the meaning of separation. No one lives here but *loneliness* – a weed.
8. 'Broken friend/relation-ships'. The words that taught confusion. No one lives here but *anger* – a weed.

The circumstances that bred questions, thoughts, and conclusions, were not caused by me yet I was left to deal with its effects – what had taken up residence in my heart affecting my life. Some of those things may have been superficially resident while others had taken root and were fortified. A lot of time and effort was used to suppress what I really felt about a lot of things that have happened in my life throughout the years. Nevertheless, all of it needed to be dealt with and removed. The rain, the weeds, and my garden taught me this. The beauty of who I really am, my substance, was hidden behind life's mishaps and tragedies beyond my control - much like the weeds in my garden. I could not be a complete and positive contribution to life until the garden of my life was free of rooted debris.

I paralleled the work I would need to do to rid my garden of weeds with what I'd need to do to rid my heart and life of its camouflaged pain. Just as it had rained for several days on my garden, it had also rained many days in my life. The power of the substance of water has the ability to make everything grow to which it comes in contact. Somehow, I needed to apply that to me and not just grow but grow up. Growing up requires acknowledging and dealing with those things that are stunting your growth pattern. I needed to come in contact with something more powerful than myself that has the ability to help me not just to grow but to also grow up. Something so strong, that the debris of life fails to remain rooted because of its power and presence. I needed to grow and grow up and until I am able to confront and address those flash cards and evict everything that lives there, it will never happen. Water indeed had made everything grow, but me.

Trying to camouflage and suppress the past is a psychological self-preservation method designed to fool the heart. But the heart never lies. Keep thy heart with all diligence; for out of it are the issues of life. (Proverbs 4:23) Your heart holds the source of your sustenance. Somewhere in the heart is a reminder that God loves you anyway. He loves you in spite of where you've been or what you've done. That's very difficult to comprehend when reading the flash cards of your past. Nonetheless, I would never be able to experience what love really means until I would make a conscious decision to learn to love myself first. The past had been a silent partner, but a conscious decision that the past is not the captain of my future that's housed within me, needed to be made. Even if you feel your past was devastating, because you're still here to talk about it, your life is obviously not over. The past has not destroyed you. There's still hope! God still has a plan for your life.

I cleaned my garden. What didn't need to be there was removed and destroyed. I plucked, pulled, hoed, and sprayed, fed the flowers, and pinched and pruned them for better growth. It was worth the labor. Flowers of various shades, shapes, colors, and sizes will bloom throughout the year. Like a good book, individually, each piece came with its own paragraph of words, while collectively, they told a story.

The results were so pleasingly dramatic; next, was to begin work on me. The truth? In spite of all that has happened in your life, God loves you and His love teaches you how to love yourself. He will somehow take the bad that has happened and utilize it for your progression. With pen to paper, I wrote:

SINGING IN THE RAIN

It rained all night in my life last night
And left me drenched, saturated and feeling heavy
Oppression showed up this morning to declare
Water makes everything grow but me.

I would have been fully persuaded
Until I took inventory of what my mind could see
I mentally traveled the former steps of my life
And discovered God, had *always* been with me.

Although it didn't always feel that way
And my faith was not always strong,
As I looked at the steps of yesterday
God showed me I am right where I belong.

Yes, it rained real heavy last night
And I couldn't wait for it to be over
Assuming the sun would immediately follow
To return my smile, praise, and strength for my shoulders.

With a slight delay of the sun God caused me to
think on the rose
And how its thorns are part of its beauty
The rain really does make everything grow
And I had to somehow apply that to me.

I've concluded I'm like the rose bush
That has a well known source of protection
Its thorns although part of its beauty, if touched,
Will quickly let you know you've been corrected.

Not anything can touch a rose bush
Because of the substance it holds,
And in a little while, it'll display what that is,
A bud full of bright color and a flower as bold.

The rose is of the prettiest of flowers
But you can't separate the flower from its stem
To do so would mean it's no longer a rose
For its beauty comes from both of them.

Its beautiful flower elegantly rests
Atop a ladder of many thorns
Meaning, you can't acquire that kind of beauty overnight
You may need to first be hurt, bruised, and scorned.

But the rain comes to touch and nourish everything in site
And gives permission for everything to grow and form
Each time a thorn shows itself remember,
The flower's at the end of the storm.

Everybody wants the flower of the rose
But no one really cares for the stem
Not realizing the stem is indicative
Of where the flower, all along, has been.

It rained all night in my life last night
And left me drenched, saturated and heavy
When oppression showed up, I simply said
"Water makes everything grow...*including* me".

Yes, it rained real heavy last night
The heaviest it's ever been
But my mouth is filled with praise this morning
Because the rose brought a new beginning.

continued

69

I learned singing in the rain neutralizes pain
And gives you strength to endure
Although it may look and feel like everything's a thorn,
The rose is coming for sure!

IT AIN'T GONNA REIGN NO MORE

My past has taken enough of my time
And I am declaring war -
For taking up so much space in my life,
It ain't gonna reign no more

All the wrong I've done and pain I've felt
Has caused enough wounds and sores
From this day forward, I'm serving notice
It ain't gonna reign no more

Lord, I'm sorry for everything said or done
Not pleasing to your ears or sight
I'm so grateful for your grace so sufficient
Having made everything alright

I learned the hard way, after all went wrong
That You're the Opened Door
Dear Lord, with all my heart I promise,
Sin ain't gonna reign in me no more.

CHAPTER 3

A Contribution to the Whole

"I'm a whole person, but I'm not the whole story. 'Set a watch, Oh Lord, before my mouth; keep the door of my lips' (Psalm 141:3), that I may be taught what this means."

I Am What He's Missing

IT SEEMS TO ME, that God did not bring the woman on the scene until there was a realized need for her. He could have in his omnipotence, created the woman immediately following the man, in the same manner in which He created the man. But God has a reason for doing everything He does and the manner in which He does it. I believe God waited until Adam realized the need for the woman so He could do what He continues to do today…meet the need.

Each creature had a complementing component or help meet of itself except the man; the human. There was none found for him (Gen 2:20) and it is my belief that the 'none found' which means to come forth, appear or exist, is this realized need. God named Adam but brought every other living creature to Adam to name. He made no errors in the naming process as God never had to correct the names. Adam had the ability to speak what God was already in agreement with. He will do no different when later presented with the woman. Everything named before the Fall of man remains today what it was named literally thousands of years ago.

When God fashioned the man after His image or His imagination, He put a part of himself (Spirit) in man, thus giving him life (Genesis 2:7). In effect, Life gave life. A body was fashioned for life and the Spirit of Life set things in motion. I believe God generated a need and enabled the man to realize the need. I also believe the help meet is for the men of humanity and not just Adam.

Whomever finds a wife, finds a good thing and obtains favor of the Lord (Proverbs 18:22) Why? Because when he finds the wife, he's been enabled to find that part of him that God took from him in order to make for him. The wife is labeled as a good thing and he that finds her is like a job well done. The word 'good' is translated as good, beautiful, best, or bountiful while 'thing' is translated as a word or as a spoken thing. She then is all his beautiful, good, and kind words spoken by him relevant to her existence and purpose. A man then, leaves his father and mother and sticks to the one he found, who came from him, making them one. He found what he was missing. He found the contribution not just to him but to his life. He leaves his covering of parents to become a covering as a husband and parent, yet they are so close to one another and such complimenting components, (she having been taken from him), God views them as one in marriage. Further, as the woman was covered in the man before she experienced her existence (there was none found for him to cover and protect), she is covered by the man in the body of marriage. Together, they make synergy in the earth with potential and purpose. It is only the marvelous work of God that can make someone from someone for someone, and their life.

God is precise in his instruction, guidance, and direction. In Genesis 1:28, God did not say be seedful but 'be fruitful *and* multiply'. Fruitful means to grow or bring forth while multiply means to increase in number. Therefore, fruitful does not equal or conclude seedful but rather includes it. The husband and wife are to not just be seedful but also fruitful. The emphasis is on the fruit of humanity and not just the seed of humanity. Humanity is filled with potential given by God to grow and bring forth all that potential says they can as well as be seedful to increase in number. If the mandate or instructions of being fruitful meant only to be seedful, where does that leave the wife or one to-be who is barren and cannot bear? What would that do to the union having to deal with the inability to do what God charged?

If the woman (wife to be) cannot, will not, or does not complement the man (husband-to-be), that man should leave her right where she is – no matter how beautiful he thinks she is. Complementing is a prerequisite of fulfilling the plan of God as husband and wife. Who she is must complement who he is before she can be brought to him or before he can find her, his good thing, his kind words. She must be a good thing before he finds her not because he found her. She must be whole and complete before he finds her because God created one whole male and one whole female. They were named one whole man and one whole woman. When he finds her, they should have one whole marriage because I believe marriage is not ½ + ½ = 1 but rather 1+1=1. To believe in the ½ is to believe you are less than a whole person which would then mean God is the cause of failure. Further, you will seek after your counterpart (the other half) erroneously thinking that's what you need to be whole. The newsflash is everything God created was created whole and complete, with humanity lacking nothing except the need for each other and to commune, relate, and fellowship with Him.

The role of the father in the life of a daughter is crucial as she subconsciously patterns her future husband to that of her father. It is her father who teaches her that men should be gentlemen. Her father teaches her what to expect from a man. He teaches the role of the man in the home, in the marriage, with children, with employment, with society, and with the church. He leads by example with his entire life. However, if the father doesn't understand his responsibility and accountability to every area of life he affects, these areas will lack in leadership and the results can be devastating in the molding of his children.

If the father wasn't to his daughter what a daughter needs him to be, without care, she will blindly seek and gravitate to any man she feels will. She will look for a man who will treat her the way she thought her father should have. As a result, she could end up looking for a man to be a father figure. The truth is, her father is not her husband but rather the example of a husband and her husband is not her father but rather the extension of the covering and protection required first from a father. If she's been hurt or abused in any form by her father or other men, and does not ensure healing, she can subconsciously retaliate against her future husband to compensate for the pain caused by her father or any other male responsible for that pain. Her mental and emotional scars will be a constant reminder. But scars are not just *evidence* of having been hurt and pained, but also *proof* of the ability to heal. Although forgiveness is the antidote, it's rarely experienced because anger and bitterness resulting from the pain would prefer she do unto someone else as someone has already done to her. Misery really does love company.

God will first prepare the woman and the Lady in her will allow Him to do so. God will make her ready before He will release the husband-to-be. When a man arrives at the home of a woman he has come to date, because she knew he was coming, she should then be ready. She should make herself ready for his arrival prior to his arrival. There is no such thing as fashionably late! Women are connected to fashion. We identify with fashion. We like to be fashionable. Late is something we have no business being but we've made excuses for it. In order to not deal with something we should, we've attached a word we like – fashionable – and somehow that's supposed to make it a good quality. "I know I'm late but wait until he sees me in this outfit." We've been deceived into thinking our fashion and good looks justifies late. It doesn't! It's a carnal attempt at making a grand entrance. It's a selfish action that defiles the characteristic of

the Lady in you. See it for what it is. Late! In your anticipation of him, get ready, be ready, and then wait on him. A
Lady is always ready.

We were made in ready-mode. God put Adam to sleep,
took something from him, used it to make something else
for him, woke him up and brought it to him. Before we can
be brought to the man, we have to allow God to make us to
become what that man is missing. Only God can effectively
do that. Single women, who know someday they will be
married, should begin preparing themselves for his arrival
and the marriage that will follow.

The male in deed is her covering but it's the Lady who
realizes in some situations she may have to cover the man
– not take over him, but cover him with her character and
attributes of herself. The man may need to be covered in
some situations that require and sometimes demand attributes more prevalent in the female. She may need to cover
him with understanding, patience, endurance, motivation,
love, protection of his name, and prayer to help him through
a situation. Not that the man doesn't have these characteristics but because of the makeup of the woman even as it
relates to childbirth, for example, some of these characteristics (such as patience) tend to be more prevalent in her. To be
the helpmeet for him is growth for her.

It is relevant for the woman to know from where she was
created before she can understand why she was made. She
will not understand that she is made for the man until she
accepts the fact that she was created in him and then made
with him in mind. She is a persona of that part of man that
represents God that could only have been expressed or manifested through a female; a woman. There is a part of God
that required a reflection and manifestation of the ability to
love, produce, multiply, bring forth, wait, house, nurture, and
maintain. The female is a beautiful representation of those
characteristics and nature of God.

God brought the woman to the man for the purpose of unionizing the two as one and being able to experience God in that dimension – the oneness of two. The man in learning the woman learns a part of God he otherwise would never know. The woman likewise, learns that essence of God that could be exemplified only in the man.

In order for the man to learn this part of God, the woman must be found like God, that is to say, godly. The same is true for the woman – he must be a godly man. If she is a godly woman, in any situation, or simply being married to her, the man will learn something about God through her. A problem arises when the woman does not know God's purpose for her life and the abundance of potential she houses. The same is for the man. The woman must know who she is in God so she can *be* who she is in God. The man understanding who he is in God supports her in doing so. There is no room for intimidation then, because each individual is consumed by knowledge of individual purpose and purpose itself carries no intimidation or jealousy.

What do you bring to the table of his life? What does he bring to the table of your life? Is it complementing or contradicting? What contributing factor can you be to his life? What type of baggage do you come with? Did you have a vision for your single life? What did you do with it? What is your purpose? What have you done with it? Do you complement who he is? Do you understand who he is? The answers to these rhetorical questions help to summarize our state of readiness. Knowing we *are* what he's missing also means we *understand* what he's missing. We are his complement. We are what he's missing – an expression of God exemplified in the making of the female and demonstrated and carried out, in the woman, who lives as a Lady.

THAT'S MY MOMMA

Unknown yet
longing not to be.
Wife, mother of all
Humanity.
Followed a lie
broke the tie
yet survived.
That's my momma

Strong yet fragile
Innocent
Covered but deceived
Wounded, a disappointment
Ashamed, afraid
Eve
That's my momma

Residence of beauty
Furnished
Substance
Sorrow and conception
multiplied
Sacrifice made for her and others
clothed in fine raiment of leather
broken relationship
no longer together
That's my momma

continued

Rejected, repented
Held on
Made it
through the storm
anyway
that day.
That's my momma

Chosen, honored
Cherished, tarried
Loved, respected
virtuous
Mary
That's my momma

Betrothed, faithful
Rejected
Delicate flower
Housekeeper, mother
Sacrifice made for her and others
Clothed in fine raiment of white
Friend-to-the-end saying
"Behold thy mother"
tonight
That's my momma

Existing and living
Encouraged and giving
Hoping and dreaming
Wanting yet seeming
To have it all
That's my...
Momma, help your children.

I Am My Mother's Daughter

EVE WAS NOT LATE and neither was she early. She was living in an eternal body in eternally innocent and right conditions. Eternity captivates or engulfs time. Whatever time it was when she came on the scene, it was on time. The Eternal God created her in the man but would use time and fashion her, in making her for the man.

I tend to wonder if it is possible that she could be created in the man, be made from the man, be joined to the man, and not know the man. How can you not know from whence you came? I am my Mother's daughter.

Hello, My Name is Unknown

Not sure where I came from
From whose tree trunk I stem
Although sure about where I'm going
I'm unclear of where I've been.

Who were my forefathers?
What language did they speak?
What skills did they house inside
Their strong bodies that were beat?

continued

What about my foremothers?
Where are they laid to rest?
Do you think their tombstones would say
Here lies heaven's guest?

What happened to my family?
Were they hung from a tree?
Did they complete the course of their life
Or were they too, lost at sea?

Not sure of where I came from
But I do know where I'm going
Won't let what I don't know stop me
Cause half the battle is knowing -

Who you are now and why you're here
Carving out the road ahead
You may never travel the paths of your family
On the same soil they tread.

But one thing is for sure
There's a purpose for your life
In honor of our ancestors,
It's time to get it right.

They suffered then
that we could have a now
we make a mockery of their strength
if we let vision drown -

In the tears of history
Discovering what you didn't know
Let's not be so angry
We can't get up and go.

Could it be I speak Swahili
And my name is Sharifa (sha-REE-fah)
Being called, 'Distinguished One'
Describing America?

Perhaps I am from Nigeria
Known for its arts and farmlands intriguing
I choose then to be called Shade (shah-DEH)
This means 'sweetly singing'.

But suppose I am Zulu
Rolling off the wheels of time,
My name would be Siboniso (see-boh-NEE-soh)
Born to be 'a sign'.

Sometimes I feel I could be from Zimbabwe
There I would be called Chipo (CHEE-poh)
For it simply means 'gift'...
What you receive, when you sow.

Other times I feel I am from
The white ivory coast
Where I'd be called Kali (KAH-lee) - 'energetic';
How I feel the most.

Ghana is also possible
For there, I'd be called a 'queen'
With my name being Thema (TEH-ma)
That's what it would mean.

Even in Israel I am Sharon (sha-RONE)
Hebrew for 'fertile plain'
The maritime slope of Promised Land
Whose soil blesses the rain.

continued

But in America, I'm Sharon
Sheri or Sharron
Fulfilling God's purpose
And living on His time.

I've come through a lot of situations in my life. And a great deal of them made me angry. Although taught not to allow anger to cause me to sin, it felt so good to be angry that I just made my bed there. It became comfortable for me. So comfortable, it became easier and easier to suppress anger felt towards those who brought harm I didn't ask for, to my life. I lived there a long time. But I grew up anyway. But did I really? Who am I? Where did I come from and through it all, why am I still here? To begin to understand why anything is made or the use of the thing, we must read the manual written for it and consult the maker and manufacturer of it. The same goes for life. I needed to read the manual written for it and then consult the Maker and Manufacturer of it. The Bible and God.

Adam, housing the human race, came from God's imagination that was based on his likeness. What God did for Adam, he did for all men. What he took from Adam, he took from all men. God made the shell of humanity from the earth but his content came from God himself. Adam was created from God and therefore knew God. The woman came from God – once removed - and yet I question her knowledge of her husband and God Himself.

We have record of Adam knowing who she was but no recorded words of her knowing whether or not she knew exactly who he was, how much she knew about him or even herself. We have no recorded words of her response to anything until God asks her a question. However, I think it safe to conclude she knew something having been created and made in a time of innocence. Adam said, I know what this is. "This is bone of my bone and flesh of my flesh. She shall be called woman." (Genesis 2:23). A progressive yet present perfect knowledge in a sentence. He escalates the knowledge of who she is in the terminology he uses. He transcends from 'this' to 'she' to 'woman'. He never had to ask God 'what is this?' Instead he says *This Is*. And because *This Is*, *Is* is a *She*, and *She* is a *Woman* because she came from me for me.

We are called a woman because we came from the man. Adam named all the creatures and their names still exists and the woman was no exception. She came from him and his seed then will come through her. It means every seed that would futuristically come from a man must now come through the woman. If God brought every creature to the man to give it a name, including the woman, why wouldn't he bring also you to the man that he might give you a name also? When a woman marries the man, she takes on his name – not his nature. He once again, gives her a name. She is a separate, whole, and distinctly different being, who complements. She complements his separate, whole, and distinctly different being.

If you're single and believe someday you will marry, act like your married now! Live like you're somebody's wife. Be true to yourself first. Be faithful to God. Learn what it means to be a wife. Count up the cost and put a down payment on it. Love yourself, love God, and love others. Learn to make sacrifices while you're single and making them in the marriage may not be so difficult. Use your single life circumstances to learn and strengthen your ability to endure, be patient, and communicate. In doing so, you're positioning yourself to be in the ready mode. I am my Mother's daughter!

More than a Woman (The Challenge)

MAKING THE TRANSITION from the woman to the Lady is not as easy for some as it may be for others. As women, we have a supernatural ability to not only house a seed but to also nurture and bring forth the seed at its appointed time. The appointed time is determined by the seed and not who or what houses the seed. Patience therefore, is within the very fiber of our being. No matter how long it takes, we have the ability to wait on it. No matter what it takes, we can do it. No matter what the obstacle, we can handle and overcome it. What is necessary to overcome, lies beneath what we see and sometimes know about ourselves.

Purpose is the meaning of our existence while vision is direction to fulfill the purpose. Provision is encompassed by vision and is released as you begin to fulfill the vision. To begin, an awareness and understanding that it's no mistake you are female and then a woman, must take place in the mind and then gravitate to the heart. At that point, it becomes matters of the heart and becoming a Lady is then by choice. A missing link in the life of a woman is that she never makes the transition to become a Lady. If the female is never taught what it means to be a woman and the essence she houses, she'll never be challenged to become a Lady.

A woman is limited in her effectiveness, getting some things accomplished simply by *what* she says. A Lady, on the other hand, can change the world by how she lives – living the life she speaks about as a woman. The woman doesn't dictate to the Lady, the Lady dictates to the woman. The Lady controls the woman and when this role is reversed, and the woman controls the Lady, I believe it becomes far too easy for the woman to function out of place. Any time the Lady is suppressed and concealed in any situation or circumstance, the woman is in trouble and the situation is in a worse state. Because with the Lady comes the wisdom to conduct herself in a manner that blesses the woman, and contributes to the situation and its resolution.

I've found that a lot of women today are finding it difficult to function as a Lady because the woman is still dealing with what happened to the little girl she once was yet still lives within her. Mentally, she hasn't grown up because what has happened to her as a little girl, has her stuck in the emotions of what happened, stunting her mental and spiritual growth. Becoming a Lady in life and its circumstances, seem far-fetched and unreal.

There are particular attributes of our self that are purposed and obvious and because we played no decisive role, they are not a mistake. For example, my color, race, birth date, and sex, were not my choice and are therefore no mistake. This is true for all of humanity. God's purpose for my life required me to be a female, born precisely when I was born, and to be of the Black race. These were external choices made by God concerning me before I existed, supporting then, the purpose for my existence. Our life's statistics or circumstances, most often, were not our choices either, yet played a specific role in how we were nurtured and matured. They were external choices that had internal affects. Who your parents were, was not your choice. Where you grew up was not your choice. Who raised you was not your choice. Where you went to school and church, was not your choice.

Since consequences are attached to choices automatically, we cannot make choices and then choose our desired consequence. They're already attached to the choice. Because God made choices concerning us for us, there are consequences attached to His choices. He has already purposed us and all the consequential benefits are attached to the purpose. Consequences attached to those choices we did not make, we cannot be held accountable. To determine where to direct the accountability, one must look to the one who made the choice. You cannot be held accountable for the actions of a disserted father or mother because you did not chose them or their actions. You can and will be held accountable for those choices you make for yourself, remembering the consequences are pre-attached.

Humanity has a divine appointment with life and have rolled off the wheel of time - just in time! It's because of the purpose for our existence, we are who we are and the challenges we face as women in particular, of any race, are simply a contribution to the vision, not the conclusion of it!

Patience ensures we'll get what our purpose designates. Love what you do and the people you do it for. For real! Understand (or stand under) your purpose, see your vision, wait on it, love it, and after having done all to stand, keep standing!

We are women of character – not a character of a woman. As women, we must search our selves, take a long hard look at what lies beneath and embrace it! We can love things to death. When we embrace what we find in our search, the love of the embrace is an important and necessary step in ensuring the roots that brought the hurt, the pain, the wounds, and broken hearts, are put to death. When the cause is dealt with, healing begins. Love conquers and love destroys its opposition. Love yourself. Love God. Love others.

MORE THAN A WOMAN (POEM - PART I)

There's a woman with no integrity -
Different from every angle.
Hosting the neighborhood gossip column
Where negativity entangles.

There's a woman who can't be trusted
Because she's not pure in spirit
A woman who tells everything
As soon as she hears it.

There's a woman who can't stay
Out of everybody's business,
Take good care of herself
And deal with her own mess.

Until she realizes this, she'll remain in bondage
Struggling with her addiction.
She should pray the prayer of faith for freedom
And announce the benediction:

"Enough of being a home-wrecker
With no home for myself.
Enough of thoughts of suicide -
Girl, think more on self-value and wealth.

Enough of not knowing how to love anybody
Starting with me, myself, and I.
And realize the greatest Love is alive
And willing to restore my life."

The abuse of a man is hard to forget
But the greatest Love of all
Can remove the hurt, heal the wounds
Causing one to again stand tall…

And be a woman with vision, hope, and faith
Reaching down to help another
See the potential within themselves,
And God's purpose to be discovered.

Selah

The Lady begins to develop at the precise moment she realizes it's not enough to be a woman. Why? It's too broad a title. She no longer wants to be identified with every other woman. She wants to stand out, be individualized in life. She wants to be an example. More than a woman.

There's a good woman. A bad woman. An abused woman. A confused woman. A hurting woman. Just being a woman no longer suffices as an effective contributory title for life because of the adjectives resulting from bad choices.

There's a woman in the crack house with no desire to live while there's a woman on the corner trying to live. There's another woman with a Ph.D. yet contemplating suicide while another sells her body to feed her children. There's a woman with no morals for herself yet she's a teacher of our children in schools. There's a woman who's unsure of her sexuality, making her unsure about everything else in life. There's a woman who's been deceived into thinking the benefits of being a concubine are greater than that of a wife. There's a woman who thinks to get to the top of the corporate ladder, she has to lie with the boss at each step. There's a woman who doesn't realize she'll stand taller on my shoulders than she will on my back. Another woman wants what's in the hands of God rather than what's in His mind. There's a woman who wants title, position, and recognition but not the associated labor. There's a woman who is a home-wrecker and doesn't care that he's a husband of another woman. There's a woman who doesn't know how to love anyone and therefore, cannot and does not love herself. There's a woman who abuses her husband and her children. There's a woman who's desperate for change but doesn't know where to begin. There's a woman who wants to keep having babies to avoid having to work.

There are many adjectives for a woman labeled by her actions. A Lady on the other hand is a woman who is careful of her actions, concerned about her disposition and affluence on others. A Lady does not want to be anything less than or contradicting to, a Lady.

MORE THAN A WOMAN (POEM - PART II)

There's a woman who can't keep her apartment clean
And yet she wants a house
There's a woman who doesn't know how to cook
And yet she wants a spouse.

There's a woman who struggles with addiction
That determines her world -
And she never really sees
The addiction struggles with her!

The addiction is afraid of
Who she *really* is
So it seeks to distort her vision
And her desire to live.

She's more valuable than she knows
Only she's unable to see
'Cause the smoke of her addiction
Causes blindness to the tree...

Of Life that gives life
And more abundantly -
Blind to the truth of herself
And that her life is a necessity.

So, because of an addiction
There's a woman on the corner –
Selling her body, killing her self-esteem
And the works of Madame Sojourner.

Who spoke of the power of the woman
And what she single handedly can do –
From the power of who she is in God
And that the man better let her through!

Selah

There's a woman, and there's a woman, and there's a woman. But...where are the Ladies? Ladies are by choice. When we make the choice to be a Lady, we'll live the life of a Lady. We'll reap the consequential benefits of a Lady.

Today's society concerns itself with the superficial because it's forever changing and change is good, right? The change society looks for, brings entertainment and entertainment brings recognition, awards, and financial gain. Today's society is not concerned with the substance of a woman that seeks to make her a Lady – that that complements the man. Rather, today's society seeks to showcase and infiltrate us and our children with a competitive spirit where we fight to win against each other and the man versus understanding we came from him to complement him in what he was called to do first.

More than a Woman (Poem - part III)

There's a woman who talks to everybody
But never talks to God.
Don't be this woman – you won't survive
Only God can hear your cry.

He'll turn your water into wine
And soothe your troubled mind –
Give you double for your shame
And free you from life's game…

Of playing with your emotions
Toiling with your will to live
When confusion, anger, and resentment
Are all it comes to give.

But God can do anything
But lie and fail to leave you alone!
"Give Me a chance to prove myself"
He's says to you, from His throne.

"You're more than a woman to Me, He says
You're a Lady of tremendous substance.
Made in my likeness and after my image
I've made you with great benevolence.

To make a difference in this dying world
Spreading My love abroad -
You've been brought with a price, I paid it all
Just need you to answer the Call."

It's not enough to be a woman, Dear
Make the distinction and be a Lady -
The only line of demarcation
Separating 'able' from 'ready'

Be More Than a Woman, Be a Lady!

All women have a past but it's the Lady who realizes her past has been utilized to make her worthy of her future, her ministry, and the man in her future. Her past can help to develop, make, and form her that she may make the transition from a woman to a Lady. If you hold on to the past, it will hinder you from receiving all that God has for you, even as a woman.

A man to be married needs to marry a Lady and not just a woman. Being a woman just makes her naturally and socially legal to function as an adult in society. The laws of this land dictate to humanity when we are permitted to do certain things and it's okay and legal. Even if wrong in the eyes of God, it doesn't matter, the law says you can do them and the law and government will support you or at the very least, declare you legal to do so. But that doesn't make it right or moral to do. Legal doesn't always include or mean 'right'.

So the laws of this land say to humanity, at age 18, you're legal and nature says to every female, at the tender age of menstruation, you're a woman. Therefore, we have two very strong elements of life determining and dictating to us what we have a right to do, who we have a right to be, and when. However, it is the purpose and counsel of God that will stand (Proverbs 19:21), enabling us to flourish. Our

God-conscious keeps us aware of His existence which then makes us responsible.

Be more than a woman. Be a woman of God. Be a Lady. As previously stated, every female born into this world, if she lives long enough, nature declares she's a woman. As soon as her body has made the necessary changes, the body will make a grand announcement that she can now not only house a seed but she can nurture and bring forth the seed. There is then, a proclamation that she's a woman and in some cultures, this calls for celebration. They celebrate the now known ability to bring forth life. We are the multiplier. We can take the seed and give him children, the same way we can take the house and give him a home to come home to. Take the groceries and provide meals - turn it, flip it, stuff it, cook it, freeze it, thaw it, and cook it again and some how make it to be what's needed. Breakfast, lunch, and dinner!

Throughout the world, women are often misrepresented, misinformed, misguided. I'm reminded of a rhetorical question found in Proverbs 31 of the Bible. "Who can find a virtuous woman?" Essentially, it asks, where is *that* woman? Where is *she*? "What does she look like?" "How can she be identified?" I believe these questions should be answered by both the woman and her husband. It is obvious where all the other women are. We see where they are. We have to deal with the effects of where they are especially when they affect things or others that also affect us. But who can find a virtuous woman? You cannot put a price tag on the value of her. Anything that's of great value is cherished, guarded, insured, and protected. This is what a husband does but until he finds her (only when she's ready to be found), the Lady with God's help, cherishes, guards, insures, and protects herself. She's of great value, housing great substance, because she's more than a woman – she's a virtuous woman – she's a Lady.

A Lady's voice doesn't precede her entrance. It doesn't announce she's a Lady, her disposition does. Her walk does. How she talks and what she talks about is indicative of a Lady. It's not the cost of the clothes but the style and how she wears the clothes. It's not the house but the maintenance of it. Not whether or not she has children but that she can be called blessed. She is honored. She is respected. She is a Lady.

SET THE TABLE

THE EVENT DETERMINES THE MEAL, the type of meal determines what is used to set the table, and what is used to set the table determines how the table is set. What are you preparing yourself for? What do you bring to the table?

A man needs more than a nice body that looks good in a dress, boot cut low-rider jeans, heels and a suit. If that's what you use to get his attention, rest assured it won't last because there's no real substance in material things. Materials things change and can be replaced. There's no security in material things. You might have a body and he may be hooked on that but after he gets to know you, the body begins to take a back seat and bears less relevance because after he's done looking at the outward, a real man needs to see something on the inside. The outward may get his attention but the inward is why he keeps coming back. A mature man is a gentleman who wants to know what's on your mind. What are your plans for life? Where do you see yourself in ten years? Five years? Next year?

What do you bring to the table? A relationship is not pot luck. Know who you are and what you can offer then you know what to expect. You don't have to have a large bank account just have one! Show the man you know something about saving. You may not have much in the account – okay - bring good credit so you can help him get much should the marital need arise. Ensure you bring something to the table from which you plan to partake. Be a giver as much as you are a receiver.

Once I received an email with a short note about women and their comparison to apples on a tree. In my own words and with some addition, it indicated the best apples (women) were at the top and most men won't reach that far for fear of falling or getting hurt. Instead, they opt to remain at the bottom of the tree, suppressing their feelings and only giving attention to those apples within their reach – which includes those on the ground. Because of fear, they may even accept the apples on the ground for convenience sake even though those apples have fallen, are now bruised, and have no luster. But they're easier to get.

Those apples (women) at the top try to figure out what's wrong with them and why they are not being 'reached for'. They lose sight of their own luster and ability to take all the heat up top and that the man must first look up to be able to see her. They sometimes become impatient in waiting for the man to get a ladder or simply climb up to take a closer look. Get to know her from where she is. These women in my opinion, are those who have made the transformation to Ladies who make no boast of themselves, where they sit, or even how they look. They need not make any verbal announcement of themselves, for the luster of their countenance speaks for them. My thought for this picture is why isn't the man at the top also? The tree was created for him and prior to both he and the woman. What has happened to him in life? Has he been hurt so bad that he feels he has to settle for what's within reach? Who told him he couldn't get back in the tree? Who?

A gentleman will not settle for what's on the ground or for what (or who) is easy. A gentleman knows he'll have to look up to find his wife because God has placed her there. He knows he has to wake up, look up, and then get up (just like his father, Adam). His fruit, his complement, is at the top of the tree and only the strong survive there.

Who are you? Who do men say that you are? Why on earth are you here? What is your name and what do you bring to the table? Preparing for the meal of life requires the right utensils. Prepare yourself. Do what you can do and God will help you to do what you cannot. He made you to be a fruitful woman, a Lady.

CRYIN' IN THE DARK

Should you turn on the light,
You would not see the brightness of my countenance
almost always displayed.

'Cause my smile has taken refuge
Behind hurt I didn't bargain for
That left me with feelings
Strong as a bass chord.

Today I cried for me
'Cause last night, I cried because of you.
And all this water helped me to see
It's far more important to break through!

I didn't know I could see through water
'til I focused on the container that held.
Concluding that water doesn't change its nature
'til it's touched by something else!

continued

My focus then was your influence
And its negative binding effects,
Tryin' to turn my waters of joy
Into feelings of neglect.

So I cried in the dark
That represented my ignorance,
'Til I changed my focus, regained my strength
And found a reason to dance.

Like water in a tall clear glass,
I stand erect, clear, and true.
What it is *is* what it is and
Make no mistake, I'm through.

Poured my water in another glass!
And my life is re-ordered.
Now I cry in broad daylight
'Cause I can see *through* water.

My container has changed,
Who I am is important to me.
And the substance of who I am,
Will help someone else be free.

WHAT IF

What if I kept myself pure
Like snow before hitting the ground -
And run the risk of being unpopular,
That worldly-tainted crown.

What if I learn to love me
More than you tell me you do -
Then you could never hinder my progress
'Cause self love would see me through.

What if you touch my heart
And I give you my hand -
Would you remember I'm a Lady
And take your place as a Man?

What if loving me
Is more than you can handle –
Are you man enough to say it
Or would you seek a love triangle?

What if who I am
Is everything you ever wanted
Can you deal with that reality
Or would you run instead?

What if I pray for me first
And pray for you next -
Then if you are the one for me,
I couldn't second guess.

continued

105

What if Adam is you
And you than, are Adam –
Then you'll cover me with yourself
In a home we'll call a Garden.

What if I keep myself
'Till you arrive on the scene –
When you see me you will know
I *am* the one in your dream.

Wake up and make it a vision
Then put action with what you see –
'Cause the moment that you do,
You're life will decree…

That he that finds a wife,
Finds a good thing.
And she that finds a true man
Will label him as king.

King of the castle and
Head of the house –
Ah, to be covered by a true man
Brings happiness round about!
So,
What if I wait on you
No matter the time it takes -
A king is worth waiting for…
A king is worth the weight.

Worth the weight of ridicule
Of not being status quo.
Worth the weight of jealousy
'Cause you know, that you know, that you know!

Worth the weight of jokes
That attack your personal choice.
Worth the weight of finger pointing
'Cause *you* hear another voice.

Worth the weight of precious silver
Stolen, sold, or lost -
My king is worth the wait
And...I've considered the cost.

It has cost me separation
To learn how to be a queen -
For the king requires wholeness
It's the fulfillment of his dream.

Before you can have a vision,
You first must handle the dream.
So, what if I keep myself
Until you come on the scene?

What if I kept myself pure
Like snow before hitting the ground -
And run the risk of being unpopular,
That worldly-tainted crown?

What if?

CHAPTER 4

Color Me Free!

"The beauty of a color is more powerful and appreciated
when put in the company of others."

YOU MADE ME SMILE...AGAIN!

I smelled your sweet aroma
that blessed my air
when the wind blew
through my hair.
And Jasmine,
you
made smile again!

Skies were grey
throughout the day
but not disturbed,
you,
blossomed anyway.
And Jasmine,
you made me smile again!

Your scent is attracting
And drew attention
to evening guests
who came to mention,
Jasmine,
made me smile again!

Your leaves
ever green
rich and full of color
shines in the light
of day and night
and Jasmine,
you made me smile again!

I watched you grow
fast
The white of you garment
lasts
you climbed to higher heights
headed for light
and Jasmine,
you made me smile again!

You have a counterfeit:
Poisonous
deceiving many
a sedative
cunning and canning;
But Jasmine, only you
can make me smile again!

Your oil
touched and perfumed my skin
blends
and cleansed my hair
and made me aware
that Jasmine
made me smile again!

My God is like
my Jasmine
to me
He
loves
unconditionally

continued

He's my sweet
aromatic
wind that blew
Whatever the day held
He
already knew.

Rich and full of Life
Eternally Right
undisturbed
by the light of night.
Helped me grow
removed deterrence
as I
headed for the Light
of His
countenance.
God,
You made me smile again!

You have a counterfeit:
Poisonous
deceiving many
a sedative
cunning and canning
destroyed, angry, competitive;
God,
You made me smile again!

Your oil
touched and perfumed
the skin of my life
blend

and cleansed my heart
of strife,
reminding me
that You made me smile.
God! You! made! me! smile! again!

My Eyes Said "No!"

Can't cry no more
over things gone wrong
My eyes said "No,
it's time to be strong".

Can't cry no more
when my heart is tired
My eyes said "No,
don't want to be bothered".

Can't cry no more
over yesterday
My eyes said "No,
today's a **new** day".

Can't cry no more
when tired of trying
My eyes said "No,
we're tired of crying".

Can't cry no more
when the sun doesn't shine
My eyes said "No,
we will *not* whine".

Can't cry no more
when the money is gone
My eyes said "No,
we are worn".

Can't cry no more
when my feelings are hurt
My eyes said "No,
that won't work".

Can't cry no more
over past mistakes
My eyes said "No,
it's too much weight".

Can't cry no more
when the way is not clear
My eyes said "No,
Good Morning Dear!".

Won't cry no more
I'm growing up!
My eyes said "Yes we know,
we've filled the cup!".

GOT NO TIME

No time for **lies**
Too much work to do
Gotta long road to travel
Before God says I'm thru.

No time for **jealousy**
Too much work to do
Gotta long road to travel
Before God says I'm thru.

No time for **competition**
Too much work to do
Gotta long road to travel
Before God says I'm thru.

No time for **hatred**
Too much work to do
Gotta long road to travel
Before God says I'm thru.

No time to **die**
Too much work to do
Gotta long road to travel
Before God says I'm thru.

Got No Time

RUNNING FOR NOTHING

Don't want to waste time running
With the wind in my face
Only to find out
I'm running the wrong race.

All the effort and pressure
It takes to run
I need to know where I should be
When the race has begun.

Don't want to find out
At the end of the race
I've been running for nothing
And took advantage of God's grace.

I'm not trying to win -
Trying to finish the course
It's not given to the swift
But to the one who endures.

Lord don't let me run for nothing
Nor step out of line
Be disqualified, and
Waste precious time.

Someone's watching my race
From this world's bleachers
Looking for an example,
A confidant, a teacher.

continued

Saying, show me how to run
Being patient with a pace
Prove it can be done –
That I too can run this race.

Someone needs to know –
It's not as bad as it looks
Just run the race with patience
And faith will be the book,

You learn to depend on
It's the substance of the unseen
Keep running and believing
It'll materialize your dreams.

God has given us life to run
Just meet him at the starting line
You'll never need to worry about losing,
He's the beginning, the end, at the same time!

He's there when you start
He's already at the finish line
He's there throughout the race
Stay focused and keep trying!

You can't lose with God
It's an impossible task
Keep running with patience
And when you need Him, just ask.

Sometimes you need a second wind
When the path of your race is steep
Slow it down, take your time
God will provide what you need.

Stay the course – keep on track
No matter what the race brings
Find a song to sing, keep running and whatever you do
Don't run for no-thing!

The race is to finish, not to compete
God's not in to competition
Throughout the course of your life you will find
A spirit-led purpose-filled life is the mission.

So don't waste time running
With the wind in your face
Only to find out
You've ran the wrong race.

A WEALTHY PLACE

With needs greater than your ability to meet
And little patience to help you wait
Be encouraged and rest in the Lord
You're still in a wealthy place!

The greatest wealth for humanity
Is sanctity and peace of mind
Wholeness and humility
In this world, you'll never find.

There is no peace without the Peace Maker
The El Elyon of everything
He's the reason for the wealthy place
For every thing is in Him.

This wealthy place does not eliminate need
But it will remove all doubt
Because in this place of rest in God
You just know He's working it out!

I'M ALREADY DEAD!

I used to be alive to what people did to me
And it hurt to hear what they said.
But I used it to make me a better person, and now?
You can't kill me...I'm already dead!

I took the things that were said and done
And made steps that got me ahead
And determined within myself, from now on?
You can't kill me...I'm already dead!

Those times you touched me and shouldn't have
And cared nothing of how it affected my head
You need to know I crucified that pain, and
You can't kill me...I'm already dead!

For all the disappointments and shame
And down the road of depression it led
Me to think I'll always have to carry this stuff, but hey...
You can't kill me...I'm already dead!

Took all that baggage that weighed me down
Got a new lease on life instead.
You see, I'm determined now more than ever,
You can't kill me...I'm already dead!

My head is clear, know where I'm going, and
Undefiled is my bed.
I'm worth more than my weight in gold
You can't kill me...I'm already dead!

continued

I gave my life to God one night
As I opened the Bible and read -
My old nature though crucified, seeks to live to kill, but...
You can't kill what's already dead!

Dead to my wants and desires
And alive to God's instead
It's all about what He wants from now on
You can't kill me...I'm already dead!

FINALLY...I ASKED

My senses were awakened by the presence of a scent
That was all too wonderful for me
It captivated my mind through my nose
While my heart pondered on what it could be.

There was something about the scent that
compelled me to search
For its origination
I moved about, here, there, everywhere
Without a clue of my destination.

What *is* that scent? I've got to find out
Its aroma is unbelievable!
It's like nothing I've ever encountered before
Not to mention conceivable.

I searched and searched trying what I *thought* it to be
But it still didn't feel quite right
So *finally, I asked*, "pardon me, what *is* that
you're wearing?"
They smiled and answered "Christ!"

Look no further, search no more,
You can get Him anywhere they announced
He's not hard to find just hard for you
To walk away from everything else you've tried.

But the more you desire Him, the easier it is
For you to walk away from the past
He comes with His own sweet aroma
That never fades but eternally, lasts

continued

When you put on Christ, it overwhelms you
And people will want insight
They too will eventually ask what you're wearing
And *you* can smile and say "Christ!"

Tell them how *you* found Him
And how His aroma captivates your life
Show them how to wear His presence
Spreading the aroma of Jesus, The Christ.

QUEEN OF SHEBA

She is Different but Fascinating
Bold but Feminine
A Seeker of Wisdom and Knowledge
Intellectual yet Wise
Perseveres with proven Patience

Wealthy but not materialistic
Beautiful but not vain
Intriguing and Self-Disciplined
A Leader God Remembered

A Woman of Character, Purpose, and Potential
Wealth without greed
A Woman of Enterprise, Affluence
Cultured yet not a culturist deceived

Thirsty for True Knowledge
Inquisitive but not nosey
A Woman of Much Speaking but without gossip
A Communicator, a Learner,
A Woman of Understanding not confusion

Admired without vanity
Respects and is Respected
Reverences God and Receives His Truth;
Therefore she is
A tree of Fruit

Royalty
A Possessor but not possessed
Conceiver
A Woman of Expectation

continued

Grateful, Giver: She gave the King
150 talents of gold equal to $3.5 million
The King's land still flourishes in abundance today
from the seeds of spices also given.

A Woman of Peace and Love
Role Model
Strong, Admired, Queen of the South
Black and Beautiful round about

She is, I am, We are, Queen of Sheba!

CHAPTER 5

Because I Love Him

"God has shown His love to us in so many ways and in so
many ways, He has been faithful. When will we turn the
table and love and be faithful to Him for a change?
He's waiting."

IN THEE OH LORD

Sometimes I'm baffled by problems and people
And not clear on what to do.
It's those times I seek refuge
Looking for answers that are true.

Can't go on living life this way
With no certainty in sight.
So in Thee oh Lord, I put my trust
Looking to You to make things right.

I read you are my strong tower
My strength when I am weak.
In Thee oh Lord do I put my trust
After Thee, my heart will seek.

No one knows me better than You
You're the only help I know.
When times are tough and people get rough
It's the towel, I want to throw.

But…You know just what I'm going through
And you so often remind me -
All things are working together for good
I should put my trust in Thee.

So, I trust you to be there for me
To provide my every need.
You're not a man that you should lie
What you declare is decreed.

You alone are God
And beside you, there is no other.
When things happen I can't understand
To your Word, I'll run for cover.

It tells me you see everything
And there's nothing you don't know.
It teaches me all my troubles
Will somehow help me to grow.

So I'm depending on what you've already said
'Cause I've tried everything else.
You're all I have left, my last hope,
I can't make it by myself.

So, in those times I'm baffled
Nor clear on what to do?
I promise to run to your Word
For in it lies the Truth.

THESE BONES SHALL LIVE

When troubles come…and they will
And it becomes hard to forgive
Take the extra step to forgive and forget; and say …
These bones shall live.

Circumstances and mishaps throughout life
Create a playground for discouragement
But 'these bones shall live' should be
Your words of hope and encouragement.

Don't let the cares of this life
Cause you to loose your stability
Letting trouble you see, hear, and read about
Take from your knowledge of God's credibility.

No matter what happens, He's still God –
Exceeding abundantly above all you can ask or think
He's still more than able to supply all your desires
When your faith and God's will are in sync.

Why sit and suffer from low self esteem?
Get up, declare 'These bones shall live'
God is more than able to help you
You can't forget until you forgive.

Forgive this one for impregnating and leaving
Forgive that one for beating you
Forgive another for hurting your children
And yet another for being untrue.

Be sad no more over past relationships –
The personalities that have clashed
Destiny is like a postdated check
Whose time has come to be cashed.

Speak to yourself and declare unto you
God is my peace and life
Restore to me joy and happiness God
Whatever is wrong, please, make it right.

Destiny is predetermined destination
But up to you to decide,
Where you want to end up after life
Then live your life as if you've died.

These bones shall live is my song and dance
Even when the music stops
I look in the mirror, put myself in check
And pull out all the props.

There's no way my past will take hold of my future
And never let it be fruitful and multiply
Someone needs something from my life
For that, I shall live and not die.

KISSING GOD WITH MY LIFE

A kiss concludes life as two
And commences life as one
It signifies that the life of one and that of another
Has come together and begun.

It means that life no longer is about being single
But rather the singleness of two
Every day I kiss God with my life
To celebrate the oneness of this truth.

The truth that He lives inside of me
And our heartbeats are like one
Each day I *do* what He *thinks* concerning me
Shining in the day like the sun.

Early in the morning
Before the light of day shines
I make a promise to live that day
With Him in mind.

Like the flower that blossoms and kisses God with its color
I too shall blossom and kiss Him with mine
Since the colors of flowers are no mistake
My shade, your shade, is right and on time.

The trees wave their branches and the
leaves clap their hands
Even while harsh and brutal winds blow
Having done all to stand, they stand yet still,
Kissing God while they grow.

The birds sing at the breaking of day
No matter how dark the night was
It reminds me to kiss God with a song
Each morning and all the day long.

The sun rises to give him glory by day
While the moon does the same by night
All of creation was made to honor Him,
And I, yes even I, am precious in His sight.

So every day I kiss God with my life
To express love, appreciation, and freedom from sin
I blossom with my flower on display
That glory and magnifies Him.

Our life to God is to blow one big kiss
Like a flower that blooms all year
Celebrating the season and the time
To praise God we're still here.

To worship Him is to kiss Him
With intimate emotion and feeling
God's desire is to be kissed by a true worshipper
Whose standing life is a reflection of its' kneeling.

Kissing God with your life
Demonstrates your destination at death
If we kiss Him now while we live
We'll live again - and *with* Him at the last breath.

Kissing God with your entire life
Is the reason you exist
Whatever He's called you to do in this world
Answer the Call, worship Him; He'll know
He's been kissed!

REMEMBER TO FORGET

No matter how many times we've let God down
Thought our way was clear and set
He looked beyond our faults, saw the need
And remembered to forget.

It grieved Him to see us go astray
And not take heed to His voice
He knew all the time what was missing in us
Yet waited for us to make the choice.

Realizing enough really is enough
We chose life over death
Our repentance of all the wrong have caused
Him to remember to forget.

He took all our wrong and cast it in the sea
Never to be held against us by Him
But we deal with the memories of our actions
While our memories of what He did are dim.

We're on the outside looking in
Trying to find any thing
That can help us win
This battle with our self.

Who we were
Fights who we've become
Trying to make the two
Live as one.

Our past wants to be resurrected
And looks for us to give it life
But since we've been forgiven by God
We refuse to be as Lot's wife.

Who turned and looked back at what she was leaving
As if it were needed where she was going
She missed out on the perfected future
Her past kept her from knowing.

So there's a war in our mind
But our heart can't agree
With what who we were
Is trying to make us be.

All the wrong we've ever done
His mercies have consumed
And because they're new each day,
Be not affected by yesterday's gloom.

Whatsoever things are lovely, just, honest, and true
Are included in each given day
To have any strength, we should think on these things
And those thoughts don't let us stray!

We have a brand new life, a second chance
To be all He's purposed us to be
If God remembers to forget
Then what about you and me?

CHAPTER 6

Well Done!

"If you want to hear Him say well done later,
do well now!"

MY LIGHT

This *'little'* light of mine?
Not so!
I'm improving the quality
of life
with the essence
of who I am -
When I began
to live
to live again
with Him.

This *'little'* light of mine?
Not so!

WINE FROM A SEEDLESS GRAPE

So many things have happened
During my tenure here
I wondered if any good would happen
To change the meaning of my tears.

Struggling to fit where I didn't belong
Ignoring the signs that said so;
Negative people, unfaithful friends
And always on the go.

Living life in the fast lane
Going nowhere fast
Trying to make somebody love me
In a world where nothing lasts.

After a while I couldn't help but wonder
Is this what life's all about?
No sense of direction or certainty
Anger...bitterness...doubt?

There must be another way
To find love and sense of direction
Who's the compass for this life we live?
Is it in a formal election?

Too much uncertainty for me
To keep doing what I want to do
I need a guiding light, a safe haven
A strong fortress to run into.

continued

So I was hand-picked by God
To be a manifested expression
Of what he wanted to say to the world
And to leave a lasting impression.

I refused to believe I was good for nothing
And that life is a terrible thing
It is evident to me through all creation,
That victory is a song you sing!

So I sing because I'm happy!
And sing because I'm free!
This world has nothing strong enough
To separate Elohim from me!

I cannot house a seed of a child
Nor nurture and give it life
But seedless grapes still make wine
And I'm still somebody's wife.

I am full of potential, promise, and purpose
Can't let that go to waste
I can nurture & give life to those precious things
This wine…the world should taste.

There is yet some good in me,
I cannot be destroyed
Seedless grapes still make wine
Everybody can enjoy.

The difference of white and red wine
Is that the skin is added for color
Both white *and* black grapes crushed and filtered,
Are processed the same at the Muller!

Determined to be an expression of God
And a role model for others
I left my circle of uncertain world and friends
Then went back to help them recover.

Pure wine is fresh from the vine
No yeast or time to ferment
But giving up and in to pressures of life
Is found in any line of descent.

I've been crushed, bruised, and criticized
For just being whom I've become
Fine wine straight from the vine,
A human expression of His love.

I'm making up for lost time
Spent living by my own plans
Much work to be done, people to help
A great charge is to my hands.

They say you can make bad wine from good grapes
But not good wine from bad
But I'm a witness to what Elohim can do;
Bring forth substance you didn't know you had.

Each grape has its own aroma and flavor
No matter what life's elements have done
Seedless grapes still make wine
In the hands of the Skillful One.

I HAD A BABY LAST NIGHT!

I was on the train
After a very long day
Had a lot on my mind
But not much to say.

Thinking about the purpose
God has blessed me with.
The importance of life itself
And my contribution to it.

I'm sent here for a reason
It's all so clear to me -
To be a living witness
Of how good God can be.

I gazed through the windows
While on this journey home
Looking at neighborhood needs
And how the earth groans.

It longs to be reconciled
And cries out for help
What happened to my beauty,
My worth, my wealth?

What happened to my clean streets
My educated citizens?
Who dropped the ball, and forgot to call
On the God who could put an end....

To the brutality, the drugs, the low self-esteem
And bring peace to a dying land?
If anybody can do all this –
Surely God can!

I thought, dear Lord, **WE** are your body
Taking you where you want to go
The only reason you're not there
'Cause somebody told you, "NO"!

No to what you've called them to do
Running away from Ministry
How can anything be changed
If the **Minister** will not see?

The old are dying without passing the torch
And the young don't even try
They're lost with no respect for life
Yet from the streets they cry...

"Help! Help! Somebody Please!
I don't know **why** I'm on this earth
Give me a reason to wake up tomorrow
What's the reason for my birth?

I know I have potential
I just don't know how to bring it forth
Tell me what I'm to do down here
What is my life's course?"

I looked up at the baby blue sky
The warmth of the dramatic sun
I wondered how something with such splendor
Could still shed light on a wretch undone.

continued

Not all of humanity knows its purpose
And the earth knows something is wrong
But the birds keep right on singing
Saying, "ha, you can't take my song!"

Purpose is like a baby
That truly must be birthed
In order to be effective
In this sin-corrupted earth.

Everybody's pregnant
With purpose for this life
I myself just remembered,
I had a baby last night!

Her first name is Potential
Her last name is Vision
To give her life and food to grow
Was my sincere decision.

She'll help reduce the cry for help
And bring strength to the community
How will she do all this you ask?
Through the mission of *MVP!

I Had a Baby Last Night!

*On a Mission with Vision of Purpose! is a South Jersey faith and community-based nonprofit organization for humanitarian services. MVP! was born February 10, 2006 with weight immeasurable!

WHERE IS THE CHURCH?

Father, what is the name of *Your* Church
and who is *Your* Pastor?
That's really where I want to be
Where Your Word is not compromised, Truth is preached
And the bruised are set at liberty.

Where Your glory is so thick, we can no longer sit
But fall prostrate in your presence
During such time there are no titles or positions
And even the Pastor has lost his countenance.

Lord, what is the name of *Your* Church
and who is *Your* Pastor?
I'm looking for Your glory cloud
The place where You are humbly welcomed
And You're agenda is always allowed.

The place we experience who You are
And hear only what You have to say
A place so awesome we've no desire to leave
Because your presence compels us to stay.

I'm looking for Your Church with gifts in operation
And miracles that can't be denied
I need to be part of an Organism (not organization)
Who's Spirit rests, rules, and abides.

Wherever You send me Lord is alright with me
Just please let them know
I'm looking for a Church whose affections
Are set on things above.

continued

Please inform the Pastor I'm not as concerned
with the building fund
As I am about the one with no food
And the family too ashamed to come to church
Because the children have no shoes.

I'm not as concerned about reserved parking spaces
As I am about clothing the naked
Those who are convinced there is no God
Because they feel forsaken.

I don't want to be where each member is seen
With $ signs over their head
And more emphasis is placed on "tithe or be cursed"
Then a move of Your Spirit instead.

Where they've mistaken a sign of Your presence to be
A big offering and emotionalism
I would imagine if there was a
demonstration of Your power
There'd be much skepticism.

Women's day, men's day, birthdays,
Anniversary, and youth days too
It seems everybody's got a day but You Lord
Is there *anything* about this You can do?

Lord, send me where there's an anniversary service
Just to celebrate the day of our salvation
The day angels rejoiced in heaven because
My soul met the Author of its creation.

The Church operating in strength and power
And every need is supernaturally met
Where we come and simply wait on You to say and do
And what we wanted to ask? We forget.

The Church where when we leave,
We know we've been in Your presence-
That darkest place in the tabernacle – holy of holies
The space filled with the light of Your essence.

Lord, what is the name of *Your* Church
and who is *Your* Pastor?
That's the place I want to be
Your Word is not compromised, Truth is preached
And the bruised are healed and made free.

Where *Is* The Church?

SOME GLAD MORNIN'!

Some glad mornin', I'll be awakened
By the sweet and pleasant song of a bluebird
Whose song prophecies a message of hope
Troubles of the day have already heard.

When the night is over and day and night
Are separated by the early mornin' sun
The bluebird sings to announce
A brand new day has begun.

As the sun sheds its light and warmth on everything
And awakens budded life
Some glad mornin' is my anticipation
Of my first mornin' as a wife!

Some glad mornin' the sun will shine,
Even if it's still possible for rain
Because in that day water is known as a blessing,
Not symbolic of my pain.

One of these days, my garden will bloom all day long
With never a thought of dying
It already knows its beauty, color, and aroma
Touch my life and keep my from crying.

I'll gaze through the window and let my eyes speak
And tell my heart words I can't begin to know
They'll have a conversation about my new life
This glad mornin' has come to bestow.

Some glad mornin', the beginning of a fruitful life,
The very thought keeps me holding on

The night has been long and difficult at times,
But I can sense the breaking of dawn!

The darkest hour is just before day
And I can't afford to give in now
Mornin' is coming on its own time, not mine,
To label me with my crown.

My mornin' is coming with the crown of my life
For which I'll be honored to care
Some glad mornin', a great life indeed,
Taking care of the crown I'll wear.

Like earth saturated by a heavy rain
So is my mornin' with love and peace
Trouble is so far away it doesn't exist
And strength causes weakness to cease.

My new mornin' brings a new day on its wings
So wide it covers the night
All I can see looking through this window
Is *all* wrong has *finally* been made right.

Some glad mornin' it is indeed,
The sprouting of flowers have began
And even the four-o-clock flowers don't know
It's only 5:30 a.m.

I'm feeling the serenity of this new day in my life
And startled by its reality
It's all too good to be true it seems,
A new life, home, *and* family?

continued

I was told hold on, for the best is yet to come
Even though I had it pretty good
I couldn't dream in a million years,
It would be some glad mornin'
that would,
bring
Something so complete and whole,
Unreal and yet oh so real
Words can't really express
How the crown of my life already makes me feel.

Some glad mornin' as the sun shares its warmth
And awakens budded life
Will be the same glad mornin' - my anticipation -
Of my first mornin' as The Wife.

UNTIL

Until the nets are full
I'll keep on fishing
Don't know what I'll catch
But I'll keep on wishing

When I drop the line
And deliver the bate
The fish will take hold
For His Great Name's sake.

Who's assigned to my net?
I really don't know
But I'll keep on fishing
Till it's time to go.

When the trumpet sounds
And I can fish no more
I'll come in from the water
And return to shore.

The commission is to catch
We have no tools to clean them
He said to leave the cleaning
And convicting, up to Him.

As long as we're here
We are fishers of men
Don't know what I'll catch
But I'll leave it to Him

continued

To tell me when to drop the line
When to reel it in
When to change the bait I use
And apply the principle thing.

The Master will check my net
And some day let me see
What kind of glorious crown
Is laid up for me.

Until the nets are full
I'll keep on fishing
Don't know what I'll catch
But I'll keep on wishing

When I drop the line
And deliver the bait
The fish will take hold
For His Great Name's sake.

Until...

*This poem speaks of the Great Biblical Commission to go into all the world, letting all humanity know about the good news of the love of God, demonstrated through His Son, Jesus Christ.

GRANDMOM SAID

Don't feel no ways tired
That's what Grandmom would say
I'm a long way from home
Yet so close I pray.

Give me a shack by the track
But gim'me Jesus she said
I gotta have Jesus!
As she'd retire to bed.

Wounded but not slain and so I'll bleed awhile
But I'll rise to fight again, she'd announce
Her eyes told the story as she spoke these words
That she knew no fear, weakness, or doubt.

All that I need is in Jesus she said
If He *doesn't* have it then I don't need it!
No need for me to worry about nothing
'Cause He talks to me by His Spirit.

Grandmom said, don't play ball in the house
Don't play outdoor games inside
Take what God's given you outside those doors
'Cause the players extend worldwide.

You made your bed hard, now you gotta lay in it
But don't lay there and wallow in shame!
Get some grit to your crawl child and get out of that rut
Life's waiting on you to be set a flame!

continued

Burn this life with the essence of yourself
Burn it with a passion for life
Light up the space where you find yourself
Blinding others to their own misery and strife.

Take up your bed and walk
Everybody makes mistakes in life
Clean up your own mess and move on
Be seen tryin' to do what's right.

I ain't tired of living for Jesus
I'm just ready to see Him
It'll be worth it all to see His face
And His glorious presence never growing dim.

No,.....I ain't tired
When you get my age, you can't be
After all these years of living for Him
Just wanna hear Him say 'Come with Me'.

Don't feel no ways tired
That's what Grandmom would say
I'm a long way from home
Yet so close I pray.

CHAPTER 7

Adam, Where Art Thou?

"If who she is can not, does not, or will not, complement who he is then it doesn't matter where he is. She's not ready for him anyway."

A SPECIAL ORDER...WORTH THE WEIGHT

WHILE SITTING in one of the finest restaurants in the world, a young man well dressed and of obvious success was approached by a very distinguished and polite gentleman. Good evening Sir, he asked. Will you be dining alone this evening? Yes, he replied. Would you like to hear the Chef's specials or would you like time to review our menu? What are the specials today? He asked. The waiter politely began to describe the various meal specials for the evening. While none of these were appealing to the young man, he opted to review the menu instead.

May I start you off with perhaps an appetizer while you review the menu Sir? Actually, the young man replied, I am ready to order. While placing his order, he was meticulous and specific. The waiter gladly took his request and placed the order with the Chef. He waited with patience, as it was being prepared, for his request was simply what he had a taste for.

In waiting for his request to arrive, the young man began to think about his request and anticipated its satisfaction. He gazed around a bit and thought about where he was, his surroundings, the restaurant's contents, the atmosphere, the caliber of people sitting adjacent and afar off. He took special note of his table setting – the grace and elegance of it all and the attention to detail. There was the brightness of the silverware, the starched napkin in its place, the water as clear as a bright idea, the candle providing a comfortable and relaxing light, the tablecloth that spoke softly to his eyes and hands, and the centerpiece of simplicity that seemed to tie it all together. Collectively, these things informed him they represent characteristics of his request. Surely the food will be great too, he thought. Everything was in its place waiting for and to compliment, his special made-to-order request.

As his special made-to-order request arrived, the young man took special note in the waiter's presentation. He carried his request on a silver tray, placing it on a nearby silver cart. The silver covered plate was placed directly in front of him and so many inches from the edge of the table. As the waiter gracefully removed the lid wearing crisp white gloves, the young man noticed the chosen china pattern complimented the texture and colors of his food choices. The young man was well pleased. He smiled.

Thank you, the young man replied. Everything looks wonderful. Thank you very much! My pleasure, enjoy, the waiter replied. The young man bowed his head and gave thanks to God for the meal. As he began to think on the splendor of it all, he bowed his head again and said,

LORD, I'M READY TO ORDER

I'd like her to be a special order, made especially for me
Help me to prepare the place
She'll occupy with grace
As we live as a family.

Like the brightness of this silverware
Let her countenance be
That her life will be a light
For other women to see.

And this candle that's softly lit
Providing just enough light?
Those times when I am blind to things
May she be my sight.

Like the starched napkin
Necessary, crisp, and clean
She'll cover up the mistakes I make
So no trouble can come on the scene.

Like the water in my glass
Let her be clear, nourishing, and cool
I've worked hard all my life Lord
For this, I'd like a jewel.

The table cloth speaks soft
Both to the eyes and to the touch
Let her be just like that, Father
Gentle and pure as such.

And don't forget the centerpiece
The focal point before she arrives
Let that stand out in me Oh God
To form a bond that ties.

Thank You. Amen.

The best item on the menu is not always the most expensive but rather what you have a desire for. The young man although presented with many options and time to review menu choices, simply decided to go with what he had a desire for rather than let the house specials and boldly advertised pre-determined meals dictate to him his choices and determine for him, his desire. The young man placed his order based solely on his inward desires and it is the finest of restaurants that allow you to do so.

The Chef's specials are simply those the restaurant has in great supply and are running a special to reduce that supply. It is also usually a meal quicker to prepare than that of a special 'made-to-order' request. Made-to-order requests take time and the knowledge of this is understood at the time of the request. So it is necessary to have patience for a special order for it is made at your request.

'And the Lord God said, It is not good that man should be **alone**, I will *make* him an **help meet** *for* him. And out of the ground the Lord God formed every beast of the field, and every fowl of the air; and brought them unto Adam to see what he would call them: and whatsoever Adam called every living creature, that was the name thereof. And Adam gave names to all cattle, and to the fowl of the air, and to every beast of the field; but for Adam there was not **found** an help meet for him.' (Genesis 2:18-20). Interestingly enough, it was the Lord God who first said it was not good for the man to be alone. The word **alone** means a separation by implication as in a part of the body, a branch of a tree, or a part of the whole of something. It also means to be solitary or divided from something. i.e., it was not good for all mankind to be solitary in one man. Or, it is not good for man to be just a *part* of the whole of something. He doesn't represent the whole plan of God, just a part; therefore, God would make a help meet for him. It was not good because there is another part of the whole of something, yet to be revealed.

In defining the words **help meet**, both words mean the same thing; to help, surround, protect, or aid.[2] It was at the completion of the naming of all cattle, fowl, and beast by Adam, that there was none 'found for him'. The word **found** means to appear or come forth. Meaning, there was none that appeared or came forth for him (that was like him) to name.

I believe in Adam's naming of all creatures, the result was a realized need for him; the same help meet first expressed by God. A desire can be manifested when spoken and it can be spoken with words or simply an inward realization or observation. As in the creation of mankind, the male had a desire that came from an observation that served as a request. Man had to first desire one that would be like him before she would come forth *for* him. The man desired someone he was already protecting. His desire was within him. But this desire **created** in him, had to then be **made** for him.

Man protected everything she was to be until it was time for her to be. God created the female when he created the male but because His plan for the female included the protection of the female, He left her as a part of the male protected by the male yet made *for* the male. The tool necessary for her making was the simple awareness of the need and desire for her from the one housing and protecting her. The male saw that all other creatures had one like themselves. However, there was not one *like* him *for* him. No one existed with sinew, hair, statue, and limbs like him.

God caused a deep sleep to fall on the man, went *in* him, took something *from* him that would designate her purpose *to* him and depict what she was to be *for* him. He therefore made the female to be the complementing factor of fulfillment for the male and in so doing fulfill the plan of God for her existence as a female, as a Woman, as a Lady, as a Wife. None of this could be until the male would first desire and then make the request driven and housed by the desire itself.

Adam and Eve were created full grown therefore, we must add to the equation, the title and position of man and woman. The man's desire for the woman was part of the make up of the woman herself. In other words, the woman's desire to be manifested or to exist, was encompassed by the man's desire for her. It was necessary for him to desire her because it was necessary for her to exist. He could not ignore his desire. Although she was not yet manifested, they were one - his desire was also her desire. It was first his awareness of all other creatures of life with their complement, that made him sensitive to the covered and protected desire for himself – his complement, his help meet, the female, the Woman, the Lady, the Wife.

The existence of the female was always necessary and evident in creation. Who she was, was hid in the male. Again, her need to exist was in the man's realization that he needed someone like himself. As soon as the man realized, none was found like him, as if to say, 'I need someone like me – where's mine?' the next thing God did was put him to sleep!

Have you ever asked God for your wife and it seemed like he didn't hear because you can't see anything happening? Have your choices been pre-determined by church, family, and friends, and then presented to you and you feel like you must 'settle' for something already on the menu? Maybe you think you have no other choice but to take the special for the day.

But what if God *did* hear you? Perhaps you are now asleep to what you asked him for. Are you talking in your sleep? Who she is, is already *in* you and God is somewhere making her *for* you. He's making her just for you! God knows what He's doing and your desire for her prompted a special made-to-order request directly to God. She must be fashioned and made just for you because she was created in you. A single woman with the desire to marry has that desire because she is desired by the man. Somewhere, in this huge yet tiny world, the man has spoken his request to God for her.

All that you need her to be is included in your desire for her. Your wife comes from you yet you don't participate in her making because you are asleep to her while she's being made for you. Adam didn't fall asleep God *caused* a deep sleep to fall *on* him. It didn't come from within in, it came from without. Make your request and then go to sleep! In

other words, don't worry about it. God is working on your
special made-to-order request!

FOR ME?

What's amazing is the man
Could not be awaken from sleep
Until the making of his heart's desire
Was complete.

He woke up knowing
Exactly who she was
Bone of his bone
Blood of his blood.

Is this for me?
The man asked God
Yes she is
Answering with a nod.

This is what your desire brought
This wonderful, beautiful creature
Although the weaker vessel
It's actually a strong feature.

She was covered before she got here
She requires that still
The woman needs protection
Ensure that remains your will.

The moment you stop protecting
Giving her space to roam
She'll be deceived into thinking
That she is all alone.

continued

She'll make the wrong decision
Separated from her head
Choosing to hear another voice
And ignoring Mine that said,

Don't eat the fruit of this tree
Or you will surely die
And what that really means is,
It'll break the bond that ties.

You'll be separated from Me
And lose our relationship
Everything will be a struggle
You'll no longer be equipped.

So Adam?...this is God
Remember what I said
Cover, love, and protect her
Be strong, *you* are now her head.

THE MAN I SEE

"Adam, where art thou
And what have you done?
Who told you you were naked?
Why from Me, do you run?

My created man is still there
And longing to be
Everything that's in,
The man I see."
Signed: God

"The color of his skin like smooth soft caramel
And lips sweet as honey
His hair, soft, black as coal
The strength of his arms means more than money.

No, you can't buy love
For who could afford to pay?
The value of love is priceless
God made it that way.

Love is not things and material gain
Rather the essence of the heart
Love without trust is lust and so
Without it, we'll grow apart.

I'm so very proud of you though
Like I've known you all my life
But that's how it feels when you love someone
It.... feels....right.

continued

The man I see has been hurt like me
And now there's an issue with trust
We have our guard up against each other
And without trust? There's only lust.

I trust…I adore,
I highly esteem you
I honor and respect who you are
A man of The Truth.

You're not my God or my Jesus
No man could ever be
But see, to me, you are the embodiment
of who God wants to be…in the man I see.

I cried in the dark until freedom came
To free me from myself
Perhaps I was the reason I couldn't see
The man for me, and no one else.

Is he my head, my covering
My loving husband to be?
Could I have all this and more,
In the man, I see?

We are more than what our bodies say to each other
More than what we've been taught
We need to embrace each other often
Expressing our deepest thoughts.

Adam, where art thou?
I forgave you for what you've done
Who told you you were naked
and why from *me*, do you run?

The created man is still there
And longing to be
Everything that's in,
The man I see."

Signed: Me

I MET A MAN

I met a man who boldly said
There is no God, to me.
I smiled with great sadness for him as I asked,
How can this be?

Who woke us up? The alarm clock he said.
Yes, but we didn't have to hear it!
We could have died in our sleep and never heard anything.
To this, he wouldn't admit.

There is no God, he said with pain.
You can't even see or hear him.
Have you ever had a headache I asked?
How did you know without a feeling?

No, I've never seen God, I said
But I'm evidence that He lives.
I'm a witness that no matter what you've done
He's able to forgive.

But I've done too much wrong - why would He care about
me now?
He cares more than you know, I replied
It was for you and me He gave his life
So our old life could be cast aside.

He died a horrible death
So death wouldn't reign over you
Instead of being something to fear
It's now a door to something anew.

But in the meantime, your life is a wave offering to Him
Expressing your appreciation
Telling everyone wherever you are,
You and God, have a relation.

It's hard to believe He exist and cares about me
With all that I've said and done
He seems so far away – it was easier to say
He doesn't exist and neither does his Son.

But what if there's some truth to what you say and
Perhaps He does exist?
How then do I find out, how can I be sure
And how can such a truth be missed?

Give Him a chance to prove Himself
And show you how real He is
He's been waking you up every morning
Waiting patiently to make you His.

Your life will never be the same
The moment you let Him in
Everything you've ever done wrong is gone
And from that moment on, you win!

You'll be more than a conqueror
Cause the battles of life are already won
God sent his Son so that you and I
Can live victorious until He comes.

You see, without God, you exist but you're not living
So your life still has a vacancy
Only God can fill it, causing everything else
To line up and agree.

continued

I know God exist but you need to know for yourself
That He may be glorified in your life
Until you give your life to Him
Nothing you do will turn out right.

God wants a relationship with you
For this is why you're here
It's no accident we've met today
Saying that, I saw a tear.

What must I do, what do I need to say?
I would like to try your God
We bowed our heads and I began to pray
In the Spirit, I saw Aaron's rod.

That let me know this man had a great Call on his life
A leader of great influence
No wonder the enemy sought to deceive
And to keep him blind at any expense.

But God has the last say
And what He decrees will be so
This man's time of decision had come
And his enemy had to go.

God is good and worthy to be praised!
Is now this man's testimony
He's preaching and teaching everywhere he goes
About the very thing he thought was baloney.

We are nothing without God!
He now states aloud
I didn't realize this until
Beneath the cross, I bowed.

He cries, come unto Him, all who are heavy with trouble
He'll take it all away
Forgive your wrong, clean up your life
And enable you to say -

'God is good and He deserves to be praised'
I'm so glad He found me
He woke me up this morning just to hear me say
God, thou are worthy!'

I thought I was somebody until I met God
And He showed me His Master plan
I'm here to say ever since that day,
I'm a new creature having met *The* Man.

THERE'S A MAN IN THE KINGDOM

Will the real men of God
Please stand up
Take your place in the home
And lead us with love?

We need you to be the Leadership
Leading by example
Mending families, government, covenant of marriage
Fixing what self and greed has made a shamble.

It's hard for a woman to be who she should
If the man is not where he should be
The family order is like a marching parade
Me behind you with your leading me.

Husband against wife, father against son
And some don't care to fix it
But *your* strength is like Gopher wood,
Too strong to quit or split.

You are durable, heavy, indestructible wood
With fine beautiful grain
No way your sons are born from you
And this world remain the same.

There are men in this life with hearts in the right place
Catalysts for change
True leaders submitting, no intimidation
With commodities exchanged.

The strength of any nation
Is in the male seed
Should *you* die…what in the world
Would your eulogy read?

That you've done your part
And it's time to go home?
Or,
that you've quit, split, and now you sit
As useless as your pocket comb -

Buried in the pocket of your death
Six feet below public eye
Covered with grass that doesn't care who you are
With no trace of your race in this place
And me *and* your children cry,
"Lord, is there is a man in the kingdom?"

CONCLUSION

Everything created was distinct from its Source yet dependent on it. In creation, God spoke and there was whatever He spoke. What He spoke was a distinction from Himself yet with a dependent nature to Himself. It cannot continue to function without His existence. God is so Omni Potent that He spoke it once and it continues to do what He spoke it for. For example, "Let there be light and there was light" (Genesis 1:3). There was and there still is. There will always be light until He speaks something else that affects or changes the purpose for light. God's desire constitutes reality; reality we enjoy today. We enjoy the grass because God spoke and said "Let the earth bring forth grass" (Genesis 1:11). Grass is our physical and literal perceptual evidence of what God said thousands of years ago. The things God speaks come from His mind and the results are distinct of Him but dependent on Him to continue to exist. i.e. everything created was and is dependent upon His existence in order to remain in existence. The same goes for humanity. We were made by the Omni Potent spoken word of God, (in the image of and after the likeness of God), yet with a distinction from God with a total dependency on God to exist. Everything will exist until God says otherwise. But *why* do we exist? And how is it I am whole, complete, and totally different from you yet I need you?

God has filled us with purpose and the potential to fulfill purpose. He'll give you vision or the ability to the see the purpose but you must maintain a passion or drive to pursue and apprehend. As Paul states in Philippians 3:12, 'that I may apprehend that for which also I am apprehended of Jesus Christ'. Meaning, we must get a hold of what God got a hold of us for! When God has gotten your attention, it is imperative that you find out why.

Change begins with the individual. Change rocks the steady beat of what is normal and is therefore misunderstood and slow to be received. It is to be prepared for and never feared. If we are not apt to change, we'll have little or no sensitivity to change and will find ourselves holding on to things that may keep us busy but unproductive. This type of activity produces weight and the mind and body (as magnificent as it is) will make necessary adjustments trying to accommodate the activity. But with no productivity, stress is the winner. Where we and others (male and female alike) may think we're strong to be able to do all that we do, the truth is, we are the weakest link because physically and emotionally, we are stressed and burnt out with little or no ability to restore balance. To be active does not always mean productive. We can think we're making progress on the journey only to find out we're on the wrong highway. Balance brings wholeness. Wholeness brings completeness.

Outward change begins on the inside. Who God has created us to be is a finished work that was completed before the beginning of anything. We are people of completeness. To manifest the finished work within us requires vision, purpose, potential, and passion. Destiny is not something you aim for, it's something you birth and experience because it already lies within you and far beneath what you superficially see and know about yourself. Therefore, we must face the challenge of becoming who we really are, head on.

Outward change is fueled by inward change. Inward change is the motivating factor but can only happen when we make a conscious decision to change or be changed. Dealing with our past and allowing God to heal and deliver us from it, is imperative for change. If you allow your past to be fueled by self pity, it will control your life, stunt your growth potential, and hinder you from fulfilling God's purpose for your life – the real and ultimate reason you exist.

Vision is, something that *is, intelligent foresight, or providing sense of direction.* It is difficult if not impossible, to understand vision for your life if you allow your mind to hold your life hostage to the past. To do so also means your purpose and potential that's evident by your existence, is also held hostage. When you make a conscious decision to change, your circumstances may not change immediately, but your perception of them will! A change in the knowledge or information base of your life or situation, changes your perception of your life or situation. Go beyond the facts at hand and get to the truth. It may be an informational fact that you're being financially challenged right now but the truth is, God shall supply all your need according to His riches (Philippians 4:19). It may be an informational fact that you were sexually or mentally abused, victim of an unwanted pregnancy, low self-esteem and ridicule but the truth is, God is a healer, a deliverer, and a rewarder of them who diligently seek Him (Hebrews 11:6). He is a strong tower you can run to for safety (Psalm 61:3; Proverbs 18:10). He is a present help in time of trouble and you need a way out (Psalm 46:1). There is absolutely nothing too hard for God and anyone who speaks contrary to that truth, is absolutely and exactly wrong.

Perceptional change is a form of vision, enabling you to see things differently. As a change in knowledge changes your perception, when your perception of something changes, how it affects you has to change also because there is power in vision. Have you ever tried to find someone's home and needed direction in getting there and when you arrived you were introduced to an abundance of people you've never met before? That is like our life. Vision gives you sense of direction for getting to purpose. Upon your arrival, purpose will introduce you to abundant potential and both you and abundant potential will manifest in your life, everything that is housed by purpose; everything concerning you, never known before, will be introduced to you. Without vision, you cannot **see** *where* you should go. Without purpose, you don't *know* *why* you should go. Without potential, you'll never know that *you can* go. Without passion, you *never will* to go!

From the abundance of the heart, the mouth speaks (Luke 6:45). What we say and do and how we say and do it reflects the state and condition of our heart. The integrity and character of a person is a reflection of the condition of the heart. Humanity is charged with the responsibility to discover and then reveal and carry out purpose. We exist on purpose and our integrity is at stake and more so when purpose and integrity is not popular. We are people of purpose and we should therefore be able to integrate what we say and do with who we really are. Our actions are therefore, indicative of who we really are; people of purpose, integrity, potential, vision.

In the Garden of Eden, God asked 'Adam, where are *you*?' Adam had in fact chose to do what God told him not to do, then hid himself and had to deal with the consequences already attached to his choice. When God asks a question, it's certainly not because he doesn't know the answer. But rather to provoke the thought or make you aware of the quilt within you, forcing you to deal with that awareness with an honest response. He confronts your integrity. The provocation alone is to make you consider why he had to ask the question in the first place! It's a provoked confession camouflaged by the question. I believe God is still asking humanity questions today. Such as;

1. "Adam...where art thou?" (Genesis 3:9); Life's translation: "Man, where are you?"
2. "Lovest thou me more than these?" (John 21:15); Life's translation: "How much do you love Me?" and
3. "...Who do men say that I am?" (Mark 8:27); Life's translation: "What is your testimony of who I am?"

If God asks where we are, then we're not where he left or put us but somewhere we shouldn't be! Further, what can possibly exist in our life that would cause us to love it more than God? Is our life a reflection of our love for God? Who is He to you?

Humanity is one race of people and that race is made up of various languages, colors, texture, shapes, sizes, cultural differences and ethnicities. Humanity has used superficial and surface thinking of these differences to create boundaries between them resulting in discrimination, giving heed to various forms of racism. Our differences should not separate us but rather bind us. We are all flowers of various shades, colors, texture, shapes, sizes, bloom time, cultural differences and ethnicities. We've been placed in one garden called Life over which God is the Creator and keeper of. He has a plan for our life evident in His purpose for our life. To ensure the fulfillment, He has filled us with potential.

Potential is so powerful that is must be balanced with discipline. Everything created is disciplined. Even rain will produce a flood if everything it touches is not disciplined to receive it at the rate it flows. It must therefore fall in drops in order for the earth to absorb it and benefit from its moisture and nutrients. As humans having been created from the earth, we should be sure of our self-discipline in order to receive the rain of God at the rate He has already purposed it to flow in our life. Don't let the rain cause everything to grow but you!

When we realize purpose is God's intentional plan, not our selfish agenda that doesn't include Him, and that we are filled to the brim with potential to discover and fulfill the plan, our energy and passion should be to that end. This is why one person *can* make a difference because each person is filled with potential to do exactly that – make a difference. It should be quite disturbing for us to acknowledge God's purpose for our life with no passion to fulfill it. Five years have gone by and you're still announcing what you would like to do. Acknowledgement alone is not enough. It requires action. It demands action. Vision with action is fulfilling. Action without vision is a nightmare.

I am evidence of the potential and variety of God. I am proof that He is not color blind for I am a flower in His garden with my own separate, distinct, and unique aroma, shade, and purpose, contributing to the whole garden of Life. I am but one, but I am. I am a complete story but I am not the whole story. And so are you! So I say to you my new friend, with all thy getting, get understanding (Proverbs 4:7). Take away the dross from the silver, and there shall come forth a vessel fit for the finer. (Proverbs 25:4)

There is an extremely valuable vessel beneath the superficial thinking of yourself. Whether male or female, young or old, may you discover who you really are in God impacting this world with the power, strength, beauty, and essence of that discovery!

The Beginning.

REFERENCE/QUOTE

How Do I Love Thee? By Elizabeth Barrett-Browning; Sonnets from the Portuguese: written ca. 1845–1846 and first published in 1850.

[2]Strongs Comprehensive Concordance of the Bible; by James Strong, S.T.D., LL.D.: published by World Bible Publishers, Inc.

Lightning Source UK Ltd.
Milton Keynes UK
22 July 2010

157350UK00001B/222/A